TALES OF TEA AND TURMOIL

by

Jonathan J D Johnson

Published by Pepper Publishing

Copyright © Jonathan Johnson 2010

All rights reserved. No part of this publication may be reproduced, stored in a retrieval system, or transmitted in any form or by any means, electronic, mechanical, photocopying, recording or otherwise, without prior permission of the copyright owner or publisher.

ISBN 978-0-9567546-0-8

Text set in Bodoni Book 11pt
Printed by Crowes Complete Print of Norwich

ACKNOWLEDGEMENTS

My thanks go to my wife Glen (a Brooke Bonder) who transferred my handwritten scrawl many times on to the word processor and who shared some of my Brooke Bond experiences in Cannon Street.

I am also grateful to Tom White who encouraged me to write down my recollections of our days working together in Djakarta.

PHOTOGRAPHIC ACKNOWLEDGEMENTS

The photographs of the riots and the damage to my company house were taken by a Chinese photographer in Djakarta whose name regrettably I don't know.

The photograph of the Tea Auction Room in Plantation House and the one of Eric Foote were published with an article on Tea in the Illustrated London News on 24 September 1966.

The tea tasting photographs at Brooke Bond's Head Office were taken by David Harris who was editor of the Brooke Bond in-house magazine 'The Tea Flyer'.

My thanks to all the above-mentioned photographers.

All the remaining photographs were taken by the author in Java.

Front cover picture - JJ on Tjukul Tea Estate.

JJDJ
December 2010

For my daughter Victoria and my grandsons Jacob and Joseph

CHAPTER 1
Brooke Bond - 1958   *Pages   1 - 26*

CHAPTER 2
Early days in Djakarta - 1961   *Pages 27 - 72*

CHAPTER 3
The Riots - 17 September 1963   *Pages 73 - 96*

CHAPTER 4
The attempted Communist coup - 1965   *Pages 97 - 103*

© *J J D Johnson*
December 2010

CHAPTER 1

Brooke Bond – 1958

I left my schooldays behind me and it was the autumn of 1958 when work beckoned and I needed to find a job, earn some money and begin a new life as a young adult. I was eighteen and a half and confident that I could hold down a job.

There was full employment in 1958 and it never occurred to me that I wouldn't get a job. Although I had been to a good school I wasn't a particularly academic boy and 5 'O' Levels at GCE was a very average achievement then. Very few people went to Universities in the 1950s. Probably fewer than 5% of school leavers applied and only the very brightest were successful in gaining University places.

I was born in Camberley, Surrey in March 1940. At the time my father, Drummond Johnson, was in France with his Regiment. He was a career soldier and we lived in Camberley because he had been an Instructor at the Royal Military College, Sandhurst (formerly as a cadet officer there) until rejoining The Bedfordshire and Hertfordshire Regiment on the outbreak of the 2nd World War. The 2nd Battalion sailed to France as part of the British Expeditionary Force at the end of September 1939.

As a Captain, my father led 'C' Company of the 2nd Battalion until they were finally evacuated from the Dunkerque beaches on 1 June 1940. Of the 130 men of 'C' Company who originally embarked for France, 90 re-formed at Yeovil after the evacuation. Many infantry battalions suffered higher casualties but the fierce fighting to keep the corridors open to Dunkerque came at a high cost.

The following quote from Robin Medley's book 'Five days to live' describes the scene at one stage on the beaches on 1 June 1940. Robin was a 20 year old Lieutenant with my father in 'C' Company.

Eric Foote, Brooke Bond Saleroom Manager

'Thirteen ME 109 fighter aircraft appeared in the sky overhead and peeling off in line astern dived down and with guns blazing came straffing along the beach at about 12 feet. It was a pretty terrifying spectacle as we had no cover but they levelled off before firing and no-one near us was hit'.

Later on, after training exercises in Scotland, my father was appointed to command the 2nd Battalion, The Bedfordshire and Hertfordshire Regiment, and as a Lieutenant-Colonel sailed with the Battalion to take part in the First Army landings in Algeria, North Africa in November 1942 - the operation known as 'Torch'. They moved into Tunisia where my father was sadly killed in action in April 1943. His individual engraved stone memorial plaque stands in the British and Commonwealth War Graves cemetery in Béja, Tunisia. My wife, Glennis, and I visited the Béja cemetery in the year 2000.

After my father's death my mother, Léonie (née Foster), was left with two young children to raise. I was three and my sister, Judith, was five. Together we moved from Camberley to Colchester to live with my mother's parents. Her father was a retired Army Officer whose house became our home for the remainder of the war. We moved to our own house in Colchester after the war had ended.

Colchester is about 54 miles from Liverpool Street station in London and I was encouraged by my mother to seek work in London because the opportunities there for young people were obviously more plentiful than locally.

I responded to an opportunity being offered by Brooke Bond and Co Ltd of 35/37 Cannon Street, London, EC4, for a position as a trainee Tea Buyer at the company's headquarters in Cannon Street. Brooke Bond was at that time the largest tea company in the world and had offices and plantations in all the major tea and coffee growing countries. I had looked at other opportunities to apply for positions with about ten other large British companies all based in London, but there was a reason why I had chosen to apply for the Brooke Bond trainee position.

The description of the prospective job indicated that the successful candidate would spend three years in the Head Office learning all aspects of the job, starting at the bottom, after which he might be posted to one of the company's overseas Tea Buying offices in Calcutta, Colombo, New York, Africa or Canada.

I, like lots of young children, had collected stamps from everywhere and anywhere in the world - just stuck higgledy-piggledy into one's stamp album under the correct country. There was no particular reason for collecting stamps other than it was quite fun as a hobby and everybody seemed to do it.

For me, the stamps that I stuck in my album under the Ceylon heading struck me as especially colourful and depicted tropical birds, plants and animals, and I found they became my favourite stamps. This was really one of the main reasons why I applied for the position of trainee at Brooke Bond - it was the possibility of perhaps being posted abroad to a place like Colombo in Ceylon.

England during the 1950s was fairly drab and dismal and the thought of travelling to a tropical country, should I be successful in my application and complete the training at the Company's headquarters, was a very exciting prospect for an eighteen year old.

As I had no work experience, apart from apple picking during the school holidays, for which the pay was £6 per week, at Carter and Bluett's apple farm at Boxted (Carter being the uncle of Timothy Carter, the tea broker), a written application for a job was very straightforward. A few personal details of name, age, schooling, what examinations one had passed, if any, what hobbies one had, etc were requested. Finally, I wrote that the job sounded very interesting and that should the company be prepared to grant me an interview I would be very pleased to attend. The application was posted to Brooke Bond and I waited eagerly for a reply.

A letter came inviting me to Cannon Street for an interview for the position. I was nervous but excited at the prospect. Mr Dallison, the Personnel Officer, had sent the letter and I duly replied, agreeing the date of the interview.

Colchester to London by steam engine was a journey of about an hour culminating in arrival at Liverpool Street station. The tunnels and walls approaching the final few hundred yards into the station were black with years of soot and dirt from thousands of steam trains, and buddleias sprouted, their stems growing from the brickwork halfway up the blackened walls. It was a few stops on the Underground to Mansion House station and then up the steps to emerge into daylight and the newspaper man chanting "Star, News 'n' Standard". There were three London papers then.

Brooke Bond's Head Office was only 25 yards from the Mansion House Underground station and seemed very large and smart. Cannon Street was buzzing with activity and it was exciting to be in the City of London, the hub of the wheel of commerce, tradition and energy - to me it seemed to be the centre of the world.

I was interviewed by Mr Dallison, Personnel Officer, Jim Wernham, Cyril Dudley, both Directors of the Company, and Eric Foote, the Saleroom Manager.

Chris Andrews, Hugh Thwaites and JJ taste a batch

The interview was surprisingly friendly, and having had no interview training, it was just a relief to me that the questions were straightforward so my answers were simple and truthful. I think I may have showed some enthusiasm which also might have gone in my favour.

I really had no idea how I had performed at the interview. My interviewers were senior men in the business and I treated them with respect and deference - not attributes which rank highly today in the 21st century. Within a few days a letter from Mr Dallison arrived offering me the position of trainee Tea Buyer, suggesting a starting date a week later and confirming an annual salary of £350. I was over the moon - a job with the world's biggest Tea Company and being paid around £7 per week.

In November 1958 the big day arrived - I entered 35/37 Cannon Street, announced myself to the two Commissionaires, Sergeant Webb and his colleague and waited in the lobby until collected by a young lady from the Personnel Department. She was an attractive blonde whose employment was terminated some weeks after my arrival, apparently for 'persistent lateness'!

A telephone call up to the 6th floor Saleroom resulted in the appearance of Charles Richardson-Bryant who ushered me up in the lift to the Saleroom. We went through the swing doors, past the two huge porcelain Chinese Urns and into Eric Foote's office. Charles was an assistant Tea Buyer who was in 1959 posted to Cochin in India, Colombo in Ceylon, Chittagong in Bangladesh, formerly East Pakistan and later to East Africa and Java. He spent the majority of his career in India, the Far East and East Africa.

A brown overall was produced, and armed with a wide broom, I joined the 'batch boys' under the guidance of their supervisor, Eddie Lloyd. The 'batch boys', ages ranging from about sixteen to thirty, were a group of about ten lads who made the batches of hot tea for the tasters and buyers, pulled out the sample tins of tea which were numbered 1 to 6,000 and arranged the batches for the tasters and blenders. Batches consisted of up to forty selected sample teas, each one of which had to be weighed into a cup, shaped like a mug, with a serrated edge opposite the handle, the weighing done by mini hand-held scales, and an exact amount of milk - a level teaspoonful - added. (Later on syringes were introduced to squirt the measured amount of milk into the bowl.) Then boiling water was poured into each cup from large copper kettles with wooden handles, all lined up waiting to come to the boil on a gas-fired range. The lids were then replaced onto the cups whilst the tea in them was infusing. A clock by each batch was set to ring after four minutes. A batch could be up to five trays long, each tray holding eight cups and bowls so that the batch could consist of as many as forty teas to be tasted.

When the four minutes expired, the clock rang and the batch boy then tipped the cup, with its serrated edge facing downwards, into the bowl horizontally so that the infused tea dripped quite quickly through the serrated edge into the bowl which contained the measured quantity of milk. The serrated edge of the cup allowed the infused tea liquid to pour into the bowl, and the lid prevented the tea leaves from slipping through into the bowl, ie acting as a tea strainer. The infusion, or remaining leaves in the cup, were then 'thrown' onto the reversed lid in a neat pile and brushed quickly by sliding the underneath of the cup

JJ giving tea talk to visiting Bank staff in Saleroom

across the steaming infusion lying on the lid. This presented a neat, uniform batch ready for the buyer, taster or blender to taste and evaluate. The steaming infusion on the reversed lid was now placed on top of the cup and squarely behind the bowl in which the tea was ready for tasting.

This sounds simple but to present a batch efficiently requires plenty of practice and takes a batch boy many months to perfect. I suppose that when I graduated from 'floor sweeper' and general 'run-around' in my brown overall and became a batch maker it may have taken me three months or more before I could present an acceptable batch on my own.

The great thing about starting at the bottom, sweeping the floor of tea leaves, then getting sample tins out, returning them to their rightful place, boiling copper kettles, weighing and milking, and being responsible for presenting a proper batch for tasting, is that when you become an assistant (in a white overall) and do the cataloguing for a buyer or blender and have learned the Brooke Bond price code (which

JJ shows a batch to visiting BB staff

to this day I still use to disguise things like Pin numbers), then you know how these jobs should be done properly.

One of the most sought after weekly jobs which Eric Foote allocated to batch boys was to go by taxi over London Bridge into Tooley Street to London's tea warehouses on the banks of the Thames (that stretch of the river between Tower Bridge and London Bridge known as the Pool of London) to collect several canvas sacks of small, brown, numbered, enveloped tea samples which had been extracted for merchants such as Brooke Bond and brokers for tasting and evaluating before the public auctioning of the tea each week on the top floor of Plantation House in Mincing Lane.

Butlers Wharf and Hays Wharf spring to mind. Now virtually all the old warehouses on the Thames lining the City and south bank of the river have sadly outlived their original use and have been converted into prestigious and very expensive apartments and penthouses - presumably with wonderful panoramas of London and the Thames.

Dock strikes and the advent of containers moved the hub of commercial shipping activity on the Thames from the Pool of London to Tilbury. Now departed from Lower Thames Street are the wonderful smells associated with cargoes discharged from ships - the produce from many parts of the world, particularly bananas, oranges, lemons, melons, tea, spices, wine and sherry. The working Thames in the City is now sadly a memory. The sights, smells, hustle and bustle, smoke, the deep hooting of ships' sirens, lighters (barges) laden with coal - now all gone.

Usually two batch boys were sent to collect the tea samples by taxi and it enabled the chosen two to have a cigarette - smoking was permitted in taxis in those days.

The London Tea Auctions were held weekly. The brokers produced weekly catalogues listing the teas to be sold in quantities or parcels as they were known in the Trade. Companies had rather exotic names - many established in the nineteenth century - such as Thomas, Cumberledge and Inskipp, Lloyd Matheson and Carritt, Gow Wilson and Stanton, W J Thompson, S S Smith and Wilson Smithett. The Thompsons, Carters, Cumberledges and Battys were all prominent in the 1950s and 1960s and no doubt for many decades both earlier and later. Splendid gentlemen such as Humphrey Crum-Ewing were well known in the Trade.

'The Army, the Church or the Tea Trade' was reputedly an expression used in the old days by fathers when encouraging their sons to seek gainful employment when they left school.

Tea brokers act on behalf of producers (estates which grow the tea) or buyers like Brooke Bond who also owned their own tea estates, Liptons, Allied Suppliers (Co-op), Lyons, Tetley, Typhoo, Twinings and Finlays.

The Saleroom senior Director on the main board of the Company was Leslie Gray, known throughout the company as the 'Chief'. Watling House or 35/37 Cannon Street had only become the Head Office since it was built, I believe, in 1956. Prior to that the Head Office was situated at Goulston Street, E1 which was also Brooke Bond's London factory. Goulston Street leads into Aldgate High Street and Whitechapel High Street and lies about halfway between Aldgate and Aldgate East Tube stations.

During the 2nd World War the City of London was heavily bombed by Germany, and Leslie Gray was at Goulston Street during one of many devastating air-raids. The windows of the building were blown in and Leslie Gray received a shard of glass in his face resulting in a diagonal scar across his cheek - certainly a war wound. He was much respected but also instilled in the junior ranks of the Saleroom a certain amount of fear - he was an authoritarian figure in Brooke Bond and the 'Chief' was an appropriate name.

I was directed to catalogue for the Chief one day whilst he tasted a batch. The assistant who catalogues does exactly that. He holds the catalogue, and his job is to call out the name of the estate, the quantity of chests on offer and the grade of the leaf - BOP (Broken Orange Pekoe), BOPF (Broken Orange Pekoe Fannings), BP (Broken Pekoe), Dust I or Dust II, etc. The descriptions of the leaf denote size. Some manufacture is Orthodox and some is CTC (Cut, Tear, Curl). Most tea is fired and therefore blackish or brownish but green tea, mainly Chinese or Formosan (Nationalist China) is unfired. Orthodox is mainly black and CTC brownish. 'Last prices' were also pencilled into the catalogues indicating what price a particular estate's tea and grade had fetched last time it was put up for sale at the auction.

The taster then tastes the tea by dipping a soup spoon into the bowl and from the side of the spoon, more or less slurps the tea into his mouth, swirls it around then spits the tea in a fine stream into a spittoon. The spittoon is a stainless steel cylinder based on a triangle of three wheels which can be slid across the floor to wherever it is needed. When about a quarter full it is wheeled away to be emptied in the 'Pot House' where all the dirty cups, lids and bowls are cleaned on revolving sponge-covered cleaning heads to fit into the shape of the cups and bowls. Everything in the 'Pot House' was stainless steel with endless steaming hot water to cleanse the porcelain (always white). The lady who ran the 'Pot House' was called Betty who ruled with a rod of iron. We youngsters all respected Betty.

Before starting the bowl and cup washing-up procedure Betty had to empty the cups and lids of all the infused tea-leaves. Far from being redundant, the tea-leaves were tipped by Betty into a sort of rubberised dustbin which was transported to the house of John Brooke, the Chairman of Brooke Bond, who lived near Esher. He was a serious rose grower and the used tea-leaves were recycled amongst his roses - a very 'green' non-wasteful procedure which would be much applauded today. Imagine the tons of tea-leaves consumed in Britain which could be used to perk up people's plants!

Each tea taster or buyer was given his own tasting soup spoon with his initials on it, so that you always had your spoon sitting by the first bowl of the batch ready to start tasting.

So for the first time I catalogued a batch for the Chief. The cataloguer puts the price that the taster has decreed that the individual tea is worth at auction the following week, in code in pencil, against the lot number of the tea to be sold.

The cataloguer calls out the quantity, the Estate and the grade and awaits the taster's verdict.

Thus: '24, Jamji, BOP' (Quantity, Estate name and grade). The taster's verdict was expressed in old money per lb, eg three shillings and eight pence, per pound weight. The cataloguer puts in 3/8d in code against that lot or parcel of tea. A full tea chest weighs on average a little over 100 lbs and a half chest about 50 lbs.

About half-way through my first batch cataloguing for the Chief, I called out "36 Dunsinarny BOPF" (sic). The actual spelling in the catalogue was 'Dunsinane' but I had in ignorance mispronounced the estate's name. The Chief sighed, put down his tasting spoon and turned around to face me - the cataloguer always stands at the left hand side of the taster.

"Where were you at school?"
"Rugby, sir"
"Did you read Shakespeare?"
"Yes, sir", I replied.
"Did you do Macbeth?"
"No, sir, I did Julius Caesar"
"Well, you pronounce it Dunsinane", said the Chief.

We then completed the batch, the Chief mumbled "Thank you" and walked away, and having left his spoon in the last bowl went to discuss his tastings with another senior buyer.

There were three Brooke Bond directors working in the Saleroom - Leslie Gray (the Chief), Cyril Dudley and Jim Wernham, both of whom were blenders as well as being Directors. Other senior tasters and buyers were Stanley Poulton, Maurice Kember, Peter Cooper, Eric Foote, Colin Walker and Dennis Porter. Assistants and cataloguers were Charles Richardson-Bryant and Terry Porter. Percy Gore was involved with coffee.

Terry's father also worked at Brooke Bond, being in charge of the team that was responsible for the upkeep and general maintenance of Watling House. Terry was married to Cathy, also a Brooke Bond girl, who was a comptometer operator in the Stockroom, a department adjacent to the Saleroom. Dennis Porter was Terry's cousin. Brooke Bond was very much a family company. Cathy's dextrous fingers would glide over the comptometer machine and she could calculate the total amount of tea purchased at a day's auction, number of chests, weight and expenditure within about half an hour or sooner. I was always very impressed by her skill.

Later trainees to join the Saleroom during the course of the next year were Oliver Nichols, Noel Boyd, Robin Adams, Douglas Fyres and one or two others whose names I forget. Oliver's father was 'The Man on the Spot' for the 'Sporting Life' - a punter's dream but fortunately for me, I didn't back horses.

After my arrival in November 1958 my first few days were spent under the wing of Charles Richardson-Bryant who had joined Brooke Bond at Goulston Street in 1954 and was four years older than I was. I initially called him 'sir' as he seemed quite senior to me and knew what he was doing and supervised the trainees. On about my second day he said to me "Stop calling me sir", so it became 'Charles' after that. We still meet annually, together with Tom White, at a reunion lunch of tea people and he jokingly (or not) tells me that he realised he was destined for high office and a distinguished career when I used to call him 'sir' in those early days in the Saleroom!

Kassomalang Tea Estate with cinchona shade trees

Whilst cataloguing for Mr Kember the batch tasting would sometimes come to an abrupt halt when an attractive young lady from another department entered the Saleroom. She would have to walk from the entrance past many of the tasting counters to reach the Saleroom Directors' offices.

Mr Kember would put down his spoon, lower his spectacles onto the end of his nose and follow the girl's progress past the counter where he was tasting. After she had passed by he would say "Mmm - big, strong girl" and then proceed with the batch. It was a bit of an ordeal for young girls to proceed through the Saleroom.

When he retired, a farewell gathering was arranged in the Saleroom and Mr Kember was presented with a fine pair of binoculars as his leaving present! He had been in India for most of his career with Brooke Bond.

The office hours of the Saleroom were 9 am to 5 pm with an hour for lunch. The Company had its own restaurant called the Canteen on the 2nd floor of Watling House. You purchased tickets in nominations of 1d, 2d, 3d, 6d, 9d and 1/- and handed in the tickets as you selected and were served your food on a tray that slid along stainless-steel waist-high rails. The food was incredibly good and the puddings - priced at 3d - were amazing, for example, steamed chocolate or syrup pudding with a dollop of vanilla, chocolate or strawberry ice cream on top. On Fridays you could have beautifully cooked fried plaice and chips with vegetables. Produce was on sale in the Canteen on Fridays and you could buy the full range of Brooke Bond teas and coffees as well as Paynes chocolates (Paynes was a subsidiary company of Brooke Bond). The Canteen was subsidised by Brooke Bond for the staff.

The Canteen was also open in the morning before work and many of us were in there at 8.30 am for tea or coffee and delicious freshly baked rolls with a pat of butter. Smoking was permitted in the Canteen.

Every morning on arrival in the Saleroom each staff member was required to sign into a large book placed at the entrance by the huge porcelain Chinese Urns. At 9 am precisely a line was drawn under the last name entered, by Eric Foote. Any person entering his name after 9 am was required to give an explanation for his lateness, eg 'Train arrived late at London Bridge'. Persistent lateness was not encouraged and regular offenders were occasionally dismissed.

One batch boy called Heaton received his call-up papers one morning and within a week he was whisked off to do his National Service. He wasn't very enthusiastic about the prospect.

Another lad decided to grow a moustache. He was told to shave it off and was given until the following Friday to remove it. He didn't and he was given his cards after lunch. You either toed the line or paid the consequences - a good system. But that was then, in the middle of the 20th century.

There was a tea break at about 10.30 am and we batch boys had tea and tea biscuits for a few minutes followed by ten minutes of Saleroom cricket using a rolled up ball of silver foil. Tea chests were always lined with silver foil and a broom served as a cricket bat. A spittoon doubled as the wicket and during one particular game was accidentally overturned which caused a flurry of activity to clean up with mops before Eric Foote appeared.

All in all Saleroom life was a happy existence. We got paid in cash in small brown envelopes which were distributed on Friday afternoons from a large tray which was borne by a member of the Personnel Department. A long, thin, white piece of paper like ticker tape was pulled out and studied by everyone when they received their pay packet to see what deductions had been taken off - a small amount of tax and National Insurance contribution and in my case and most of the other lads in the Saleroom and Stockroom a 6d per week deduction for membership of the Brooke Bond Social Club.

The club's games room was in the basement and was provided with a ping-pong table, a darts board and shove-halfpenny board. George Piercy taught me shove-halfpenny. The main activity in the games room, however, was music. There was a record player and hundreds of 7 inch EP records which were the week to week hit parade favourites. This was the late '50s and early '60s and the music was by stars like Pat Boone, Tommy Steele and Bill Haley and his Comets. There were loads of pretty girls working at Brooke Bond in various departments and they jived together much to the enjoyment of all the young men including me. This really was the beginning of the 'swinging sixties' - very short skirts, shiny nylons and stiletto-heeled shoes with pointed toes.

After a few weeks at Brooke Bond, commuting to Cannon Street from Colchester by steam train, I decided that it would be a good idea for me to live in London and come home to Colchester at the weekends. My mother kindly got in touch with Universal Aunts, a company in London which could arrange tasks like escorting children across London to meet parents or finding accommodation for people. They came up with a lady who owned a house at 9 Cheyne Place at the end of the Royal Hospital Road in Chelsea and who had a small spare room to let at £3 a week including a cooked breakfast. I went to see the room with my mother and decided that it would suit me well and I moved in. Edome Sharpe, née Broughton-Adderley, was the owner and she could also provide an evening meal for 5/- if you required it but you needed to request the evening meal at breakfast time. Her breakfast scrambled egg on toast was the best I've ever tasted. I've never succeeded in reproducing it to her standard.

Mr Sam, P & T botanist - Kassomalang Estate

The Broughton-Adderley's country house in Sussex was called 'Peppers'. Edome said that the lake was full of empty brandy bottles thrown in by her father! She had two children, Rowena and Stephen. Rowena was a bright young teenager whose best schoolfriend at the Francis Holland School was called 'Cordelia' - a strange name I thought to call a girl. Rowena went on to marry David Grant, of the Grant whisky family. David, whom I knew well, was an exact contemporary of mine at Rugby, in the same House, School Field, for 5 years and joining the same term. Stephen was sadly killed in a car accident when he was about 20.

A walk of perhaps three quarters of a mile took me from Cheyne Place along the Royal Hospital Road past the Royal Hospital and its beautiful grounds and towards Sloane Square. Large ticket machines looking like one-armed bandits with lighted glass indicating 3d or 6d fares stood on both sides of the central ticket office which was manned on both sides for those queuing who didn't have the correct change for the machines. Pennies and half-pennies, farthings, threepenny pieces, sixpences, shillings, two shilling pieces (known as florins) and half-crowns were the coins of those days before decimalisation, and the notes were ten shillings and one pound. Five pound notes, called 'flimsies', were not seen very often by the ordinary public but they were white, rather large and folded up. Some prices were still quoted in guineas – twenty-one shillings.

It is seven stops on the Circle and District line between Sloane Square and Mansion House and often the sun would be shining onto the platform as the train arrived and as the doors opened, a huge cloud of grey-blue cigarette smoke would curl out and float up into the sky. The tube train was usually made up of around eight smoking compartments and one non-smoking. How times have changed.

Towards the end of 1960, when I had become proficient at batch-making and cataloguing and other Saleroom procedures, Jim Wernham asked me to pop into the blending room to see him. He explained that Colin Hammond, of Francis Peek and Co, one of Brooke Bond's subsidiary companies, had become very busy and had approached Jim Wernham to ask if he could spare someone from the Saleroom to go and become his assistant at the Francis Peek office in Eastcheap, just near the Monument. Jim thought that I would make a suitable candidate and arranged a meeting between himself, Colin Hammond and me. I wasn't that keen on the idea as I didn't really want to leave working in the Saleroom where I was very happy and particularly because of the companionship and hustle and bustle that working there entailed. Also I would miss trips up to Plantation House to visit the Tea Auction in order to collect catalogues from our broker SS Smith to return to the Chief for him to see how much tea was being bought on that particular day. It was also interesting and entertaining to sit in the comfortable large, brown leather tip-up seats in the Tea Auction auditorium next to our broker and follow him buying, or sometimes splitting a parcel of tea. Splitting was when say 60 chests were offered - the bid was with our broker. Harrisons might ask for 30 chests and if agreed both brokers would get 30 chests each for their respective clients, Brooke Bond and Typhoo, at the indicated price. If Smiths didn't wish to let Harrisons have 30, Harrisons would bid on and the price would rise until the hammer fell and the lot was allocated to the successful bidder.

Although I didn't know Colin Hammond personally, I knew him by sight as almost every day I would see him lunching in the Canteen in the serviced section. For a small amount extra you could have waitress service and most of the senior tea buyers, accountants and lawyers in the Company would avail themselves of that service. The Directors of Brooke Bond lunched in their own separate dining room.

Francis Peek, originally called Peek Bros & Winch, were the London agents of The Anglo-Indonesian Plantations of Java and several other plantation companies in Java, Sumatra and Borneo (Kalimantan). Colin Hammond's father, E J Hammond had long been a senior man, originally with Peek Bros & Winch, in AIP which in Java was known as Pamanoekan and Tjiasem Lands, or P & T Lands. In about 1910 he oversaw the expansion of P & T Lands to include tea, rubber, coffee, sisal, rice, tapioca, pineapples, teak and balsawood, pepper, spices, cinchona and sugar. Also grown on the Lands in 1909 were quite substantial quantities of mace, nutmegs, vanilla, cassia, aloes, coconuts, derris (used in the production of sheep-dip) and kapok. The Lands were spread across something in the nature of half a million acres in 1900. P & T Lands could also claim its own volcanoes on the then coffee estate called Soekaboemi. On part of the 3,700-acre estate were the slopes of the Merapi (Red Fire) and the Merbaboe. Merapi is one of the most active of the Java volcanoes. 'This grim custodian keeps perpetual watch over the estate and there are comparatively few days when the eruption of smoke does not act as a reminder of its lurking menace' to quote Wilfred H Daukes in 1926 (Chairman and Managing Director of the Anglo-Indonesian Plantations of Java Ltd.) * *See note at end of chapter.*

As a consequence of our meeting in Jim Wernham's office it was decided that I would go and work as Colin Hammond's assistant in Eastcheap. I would still be paid by Brooke Bond and continue to enjoy the benefits that were enjoyed by other Brooke Bond staff including having lunch in the Canteen at Cannon Street and meeting up with my Saleroom colleagues.

An old-fashioned lift with two grill-barred gates which were closed with a crash and clunk was a feature inside the entrance to the office building in Eastcheap. Mr Lindsell operated it. Lindsell had a large white moustache and I suspect had been with Francis Peek for many years because he ruled in imperious style, much to the amusement of all

Tea Auction, Plantation House
Centre row - James Fellows, Tom Corley, JJ
Front row - Tom King

who met him daily on arrival at the office. His number two was a small man called Feaney. He was in charge of the boiler room and he and Lindsell brought morning tea round at eleven o'clock.

Feaney was an Irish republican, spoke with a broad Irish brogue and used to greet me with "H'up the IRA!" I liked Feaney and used to help him rake out the huge boiler in the basement, revealing large, red hot clinkers. I would then shovel in quantities of coke on a wide-based shovel. I think he appreciated me helping him in the boiler room.

Sometimes during the summer after lunch I would go up onto the roof of 5/7 Eastcheap and sit on a lead-lined perch amongst the wonderful array of chimney pots of all shapes and sizes which crowned all the old buildings around. I often thought that the roofs and chimney pots would be an excellent subject for an artist to paint.

The work was somewhat different but still included batch making for the tasting of samples of the AIP teas sent from Djakarta. Francis Peek, as agents, controlled the sale of all the tea and rubber and sent directions to the Djakarta office by telegrams which were always translated into code using the Bentleys 2nd Code system. The first words normally started 'May we sell ...' for which the code word was 'Twemy'. I am still not clear why

Gunung Salak on the road from Puntjak Pass to Djakarta

the telegrams needed to be coded. The price of Java tea for sale on the market was not exactly a state secret. The telegrams which went overnight to Java were collected from the Post Office in Djakarta by someone on their way into the office at Kali Besar Barat in the Kota district. The telegrams then had to be de-coded in the Djakarta office of Francis Peek and the contents acted upon. The Bentleys Code book was very large, heavy and well-worn.

James Fellows, a Brooke Bond man, was the manager of the Francis Peek Djakarta Tea Department.

Tom White whom I had met briefly at Francis Peek had gone out to the Djakarta office, shortly followed by his wife Jackie, all of whom I was later in 1961 to get to know well.

Colin Hammond was a very congenial boss and we smoked in his small office. The Chairman of Francis Peek was a charming elderly gentleman called Jen Nathan who visited Colin Hammond's office nearly every morning, usually smoking a cigar, to ask us if we knew the answer to a particular question in The Times crossword which had so far eluded him. I think he was wasting his time for I never recall either Colin Hammond or myself ever having assisted Mr Nathan in his request for a correct answer to his crossword clue. He normally had it finished by lunchtime.

Colin Hammond's daughter was called Celia. I had dinner one evening with Colin, his wife Enid and Celia in Hampstead where they lived. Celia was then working at Harrods of Knightsbridge in the Pet Department. She loved animals. A very beautiful girl, she soon afterwards went into modelling to become the famous model, Celia Hammond, a contemporary of Jean Shrimpton. For a long time her boyfriend was Dudley Moore, the entertainer, pianist and actor.

After finishing her modelling career Celia devoted her life to animal welfare. Her organisation has clinics in Canning Town and Lewisham plus a sanctuary in East Sussex housing cats and dogs awaiting re-homing. Full veterinary services are available at the clinics. She is a remarkable lady. The Celia Hammond Animal Trust (CHAT) headquarters is based in Wadhurst (East Sussex).

In the summer of 1961 I was finishing my lunch in the Brooke Bond Canteen with a few colleagues when someone came up to the table with a message for me saying that Mr T D Rutter, the Brooke Bond Deputy Chairman, would like to see me in his office on the 5th floor at 2 pm.

I was surprised and not a little anxious to be summoned to the Brooke Bond corridor of power. Mr Rutter was, of course, well known in the Company and as deputy to the Chairman, John Brooke, held considerable power. I wondered whether I might have committed some misdemeanour or other so it was with some considerable trepidation that I knocked on the door and entered his office.

He told me to sit down and then went on to explain that Brooke Bond had decided to close down the Francis Peek agency in Djakarta (for reasons that were not mentioned and to this day I don't know why) and that Jimmy Fellows would be returning to London. Tom White was to become the Manager of the office which would be transferred into the direct ownership and direction of the Anglo-Indonesian Plantations whose head office was at Subang near Bandung where most of the tea and rubber estates were situated. The tea estates were at a higher elevation than Subang, about twenty miles distant on the foothills and lower slopes of the great volcano 'Tankoeban Prahoe' which translated means 'overturned boat'. The volcano has two craters, the upper and lower, some miles apart

A Prahu off Java

which explains the name. The craters face north overlooking the Lands. There was a serious eruption in 1910 and although violent activity is rare, the craters' smouldering presence are a reminder of the danger from the 'ring of fire', a volcanic chain, which stretches like a coral necklace from Japan through the length of South East Asia, passing right through Sumatra, Java, Bali, Lombok and on to Irian (Dutch New Guinea, now part of Indonesia.)

Mr Rutter explained that the closing of Francis Peek's Djakarta office meant that the Anglo-Indonesian Plantations didn't have a tea man in Djakarta to supervise the export of all their tea production through the port of Tandjong Priok, just outside Djakarta, and he would like me to fulfil that role in Java.

The following day I received a letter from Mr Rutter outlining our discussion and agreeing to re-appoint me as an assistant in the London Brooke Bond Saleroom should conditions in Java change to a situation when I would no longer be able to work there. He understood the fragile political events which were unfolding in Indonesia. All Dutch nationals had been expelled in 1958.

Tjukul Tea Estate, Java, 1962

It was therefore decided that I would be transferred directly into the employ of the AIP and because I was young, a mere 21, I would be appointed to the position of under-manager of the Tea Department of the AIP in Djakarta, subject to obtaining a work permit. James Fellows would remain in Djakarta to instruct me in the tea export procedures for about 6 weeks before handing over to me and then returning to London where he would become Brooke Bond's tea broker with S S Smith (which Brooke Bond owned). I believe that Mr Rutter's family had owned S S Smith at one time.

Like Tom White, who was aged 26, I would therefore be employed by the AIP in Java and they would advise me of the terms and conditions of employment and also they would pay my salary, both in sterling in England and in rupiahs in Java. This dual arrangement of a small monthly sterling payment in London and rupiah payment locally was because rupiah inflation was rampant and expatriates in Indonesia were not permitted to hold foreign currency of any description. My rupiah salary when I arrived in Java in 1961 was 9,000 per annum and when I was finally ousted in June 1964 it was 2.5 million rupiahs per annum - inflation with long strides.

Hammond receiving the insignia of "Officer of Oranje Nassau" from the Resident of Batavia.
[Photograph by "Charls & van Es & Co."]

E J Hammond, 1923

The work permit was expected to take some time to arrange and in the meantime Richard Shaw, the Representative (Chief) in Subang, wrote to me setting out all the details - a contract of three and a half years with six months' home leave after that period. A house, servants, car and driver, various allowances (including 6 golf balls and a bottle of whisky and gin per month) would all be provided for me without cost. The reason for golf balls, whisky and gin as monthly allowances was because of Indonesia's dire economic circumstances. Imports of luxury European goods were severely restricted and often only obtainable at hugely inflated prices on the open market.

Colin Hammond, like his father before him who went out to Java originally in 1909, had also spent many years in Java with Francis Peek and told me that when he was in the East he did five year tours and that he thought I was lucky to have as little as a three and a half year tour.

Colin's father, E J Hammond, had for many years been Managing Director and Representative in Java and had been a far-sighted and energetic leader of the P & T Lands as well as Francis Peek. He was in 1923 created by the Queen of the Netherlands an Officer of the Order of 'Oranje Nassau' receiving the insignia from the Dutch Resident of Batavia (now Djakarta).

Mr G C Denham from Singapore had taken over the management in Subang from E J Hammond in January 1926. The latter returned to the Board in London but his health was declining and he sadly died in August 1926 before he could take up the Chairmanship of the Company.

---

*Just before 'Tales of Tea and Turmoil' went to Crowes in Norwich to be printed, reports came through from Java that the Merapi volcano had erupted on 25 October 2010. A tsunami sweeping in over islands on the coast of Sumatra was also reported on the same day. Dramatic television film of Merapi and the inundated islands was broadcast on BBC News across Britain the following day. Both these events which occur intermittently in this region of the world have resulted in tragic loss of life.

The latest tsunami is the consequence of another seismic movement in the same subterranean fault which caused the catastrophic tsunami in 2004 when around 230,000 people died. It is a reminder that turmoil is constantly simmering not only beneath the earth but also upon it in these unpredictable times.

JJ at the company bungalow in the hills, 1962

CHAPTER 2

Early days in Djakarta – 1961

Dr Sukarno was the President of Indonesia. He was a colourful fellow who was instrumental in forming the Republic of Indonesia after World War II and for declaring independence from the Dutch in 1945.

I now quote from Tarzie Vittachi's book 'The Fall of Sukarno' published by Mayflower Books Limited in 1967:

'The opening words of his (Sukarno's) autobiography are:

'The simplest way to describe Sukarno is to say that he is a great lover. He loves his country, he loves his people, he loves women, he loves art and, above all, he loves himself'.

This thumb-nail sketch was Louis Fischer's, not Sukarno's own, but he himself has frequently used it without the formality of quotation marks, and he evidently likes it as an image of himself.'

I quote again from the same source:

'A reporter once asked him what he had given his country except poverty, disease and corruption, and he answered angrily: "I'll tell you what I have done for my country. I have transformed our islands into one nation. This archipelago was inhabited by Javanese, Sumatrans, Sulawesis, Sundanese and so on; Muslims, Christians, Hindus, animists - different cultures, traditions, languages, religious beliefs. Now they are all Indonesians. Is that not an achievement"?'

It is true that he really did give his people a sense of pride in their nationality. Sukarno saw to it that the journalist never worked in Djakarta again.

My passport photos had been required to be sent to Java to enable the work permit to be processed. Colin Hammond surprised me by suggesting that I should have 50 printed as such things as radios needed a permit, and all permits, driving licence, resident's permit etc, required photos. He was right.

I had plenty of time to purchase most of the clothes required for working in the tropics - cotton was the material required for underwear, socks, shirts and trousers - never nylon. Airey and Wheeler of Piccadilly were London's tropical outfitters and most of my things came from there. I intended to travel with two Revelation suitcases and the rest of my things would be packed in a 'lift-van' and go to Java by sea - golf clubs, cricket gear, gramophone, records, etc. I would travel by air from Heathrow to Djakarta by Comet IV, BOAC's main long-distance jet airliner which would make seven re-fuelling stops on the way. Each stop would be for approximately one hour and passengers had to disembark and go into a 'transit lounge'.

I had to make a visit to the Brooke Bond private Doctor's practice in Harley Street to have a medical to see if I was fit to work in the tropics. He asked if I played cricket and explained that a games player would be quite useful for the Anglo-Indonesian Plantations of Java as they played a bi-annual games contest against the British American Tobacco Company which consisted of competitive golf, cricket, tennis and snooker. The Doctor gave me a rudimentary health check and declared me fit to work in Java.

Banka Tin pint tankards with 'BAT v P & T' engraved on them were presented to each member of the winning team. Banka Tin was like silver and came from Banka Island off the north-east coast of Sumatra due north of Palembang. Both Tom and I won an engraved tankard in 1962.

A trip to Victoria Street was also necessary to attend the BOAC building opposite the Victoria Bus Station where an inoculation book was produced and into which the required injections and inoculations which I was given were recorded. Cholera, TAB and smallpox boosters would be required every six months in Djakarta and would be administered by Dr Furlong, a British doctor attached to the British Embassy, whose practice in Djakarta was funded by the Embassy and the British Companies operating in Java. The TAB injection resulted in an extremely sore left upper arm and for a few days felt as if my arm had been hit by a hammer. Driving a car was especially painful, in particular turning the steering wheel.

Charles Jackson, the Chairman of the AIP, called me in before I finally departed from the Eastcheap office and said to me "Don't forget that while you are in Java you represent not only the company but also your country". Mr Jackson went to Java from South India in 1922 to look after rubber production of the P & T Lands and was appointed Representative at Subang in 1941. He was interned when the Japanese invaded in 1942. He spent the remainder of the war in a Japanese prison camp. He was an example of a true gentleman. Tall, slim, quiet and courteous, with large, thick horn-rimmed spectacles, he was greatly respected.

Colin Hammond and my mother kindly came to Heathrow to see me off as well as my Aunt Edith and Uncle Cyrus Greenslade. I had only flown in BEA propeller planes before this, so to fly on a Comet jet was a new and exciting event.

We refuelled in Rome, Beirut, Karachi, Calcutta, Bangkok and Singapore finally landing at Kemajoran Airport outside Djakarta. As we had landed in Calcutta around 6 in the morning, it wasn't very hot, although I noticed with some alarm a large number of vultures squatting on the hangars of Dum Dum airport. But on getting off the Comet at Singapore, my trousers were clinging to my legs as I descended the aircraft steps down to the tarmac. I thought that the heat must be coming from the Rolls Royce engines which you pass on the way down the gangway steps. On walking across the tarmac to the 'transit lounge' at Singapore Airport, the temperature remained the same and it was at that moment that I realised that I had arrived in a tropical climate. Yes, it was hot, just as Colin Hammond had described.

The flight had been fine, I had had a little sleep, and there were some flashes of lightning around from time to time. I'd enjoyed a meal or two and the Comet was only about half full so I had a window seat and the seat next to the aisle was empty. The plane was flying on to Sydney so there were a number of Australians on board.

Arriving at Kemajoran Airport at about 5 pm, I was met by Tom White and Tukan, an Indonesian assistant, to help with customs and any other formalities. The police and military were in evidence, with white leather holsters and pistol butts poking out from them but all were very friendly and soon we were ushered through the formalities and out of the building.

Tom White's driver, Usen, brought Tom's Chevrolet 'Bel Air' to pick us up and we set off to drive to Djakarta. It was still light and we drove alongside a river in which floated great swathes of water-hyacinth looking like large clumps of entangled ivy with blue flowers crowning the green leaves.

A dusty haze seemed to rise from the none too smooth road but the 'Bel Air' rode the bumps and uneven surface with no problem. Usen was a good-natured fellow, a youngish, black-haired Javanese, dressed in a white shirt and white drill trousers with a black Kopiah (velvet cap) on his head. He had a friendly smile on his face and he obviously enjoyed driving 'his' Bel Air and was constantly polishing and buffing the chrome and body paint. The colour was silvered russett red with cream running lines from fore to aft. It was a fine mid-1950s American car with lots of sparkling chrome, built for comfort and capable of riding the pot holes and bumps. The Bel Air's springs were built to last and Usen nursed the car avoiding the worst of the pot holes.

The car followed the route into the outskirts of Djakarta which bustled with activity. Strange sights, bright colours and unusual smells on the tropical air were all exciting to me and I didn't feel tired even after my long journey.

It was at around dusk that Usen drove down Djalan Borobudur and into the drive of the fine looking house at the end of the road on the right hand side. Tom and Jackie White's address was Djalan Borobudur 2, Pegansaan, Djakarta. The Box Club was straight ahead of it. Jim Wernham had mentioned the Box Club to me, remembering it from his younger days in Java, but he called it the 'Box and Cox'! It was actually the British Cricket Club.

Jackie White, Tom's wife, greeted me and took me upstairs to show me where I would be sleeping. It was a comfortable room with storm shutters attached to the outside of the windows. Fine wire mesh on swing frames covered the interior of the windows. This was called 'fly-wire' and prevented mosquitoes entering but also allowed the flow of air, if there was any wind, into the room. There was no glass in any of the windows - normal in the tropics then - before houses had air-conditioning. The door into the bedroom was also 'fly-wired'. Mosquitoes in the bedroom were not encouraged and on the tiled floor was a hand pump-action device with a cylindrical container the size of a Coca Cola can attached to a two foot handle. It was called 'Pumpa Flit' and by pump action a fine spray of Flit could be directed round the room to kill any mosquitoes which had managed to penetrate the defences during the day. Hanging down from the ceiling was the kepas - the fan which usually had three speeds. One should remember that air-conditioning was in its infancy and the normal air cooling movement which had succeeded hand or foot controlled 'punkahs' had become the large ceiling fan which was called a 'kepas' in Java.

When I had changed out of my travelling clothes, had showered and generally tidied myself up, I came downstairs into the large open-plan sitting room area. Comfortable armchairs, sofas and a big coffee table were arranged at one end of the room and the dining area adjoining.

These large houses were planned to be as airy as possible so upon entering through the main entrance door, the large lobby led directly into the sitting room and dining area - no doors - the entire floor area paved

Djalan Borobudur 2, Tom and Jackie White's house, my Fiat

with tiles. The staircase was also open-plan leading up from the lobby with another sofa and chairs at the foot of the stairs.

We sat down before supper for a drink and some nuts - 'kachang merah' rather like dark red peanuts in salt - very tasty. On special occasions frogs' legs with salt and lemon juice were sometimes provided - I loved them. At the side of the window behind the sofa hung a little row of small tubular wind-chimes which softly jingled in the slight tropical breeze - a memorable and soothing sound.

Tom, Jackie and I sat down at the dining table. The cook, Isa, a lovely Javanese, looking probably somewhat older than she really was, served an excellent meal. Tom and Jackie's dinner service was Noritake china and needed handling with care. Tatang, the houseboy, helped serve and was there to replenish drinks and clear away as required. Maan was houseboy number two. The servants were charming and very polite and I was already beginning to feel at home in this new tropical environment in which I found myself.

It was on a Sunday that I had arrived in Djakarta and Jackie mentioned whilst we were eating that there was a film on at the 'Box Club' that

The side garden of Djalan Borobudur 2

evening and would I like to go with them to see it? Films at the Box were always on Sunday evenings and very popular as English and American films were not readily available and were even banned from showing in the local cinema (Bioscop Menteng).

The Box Club was the name generally used for the British Cricket Club which happened to be almost next to the Borobudur house. You went through a wicket gate at the rear of the property over the small road, Djalan Borobudur, and then directly onto the gravel car parking area of the Box Club.

The Club was a single storey building, with wide wooden steps leading up onto a balcony and entrance. The balcony, at waist height, was decking which ran along two sides of the building on the entrance side and on the longer side which faced the playing fields and tennis courts. Tables and chairs were arranged all along the balcony. Inside on the left as you entered was the Secretary's Office which led through to the long bar on the left and then the main indoor area of the Club which doubled as a dance floor or auditorium with rows of chairs to watch a film, or tables and chairs for a bingo evening. At the end of the hall there was a stage in front of which the screen was erected for Sunday film nights. At the rear were changing rooms and a dining room with bar. There was also a fine snooker room which was very popular.

On film nights the Club was packed. There were a few Indonesian members of the Box but on the whole the membership was British, Australian, New Zealand, Scandinavian, a few Americans and Italians.

The extent of the grounds was probably about two and a half acres, the boundary delineated with neat hedgerows and Djalan Borobudur, the road, ran round to the right of the Club entrance then left and left again enclosing the Club on three sides.

It had become dark by the time we left the house to cross the road via the wicket gate at the rear to the Club entrance - only a matter of yards away to see the film. Wooden criss-crossed planks led from the gate onto the road but unknown to me was a small ditch with water at the bottom into which I side-stepped off the wooden planks. I slipped into the ditch, said "bother" and climbed out, my shoes a bit wet.

We took our seats for the film, a full house, barboys serving drinks. It was fairly hot in the Club and I saw in front of me a few rows ahead a tall, large man who had been on the same Comet flight from London and had also disembarked at Djakarta. I recall that he was Alan Mays-Smith who had arrived to work for Shell. Lots of small boys from the kampongs in the area came onto the outside balcony and clung to the security bars which went down to balcony level, poking their heads through the bars to watch the film with much excitement.

We all enjoyed the film, my first introduction to the Box Club, and retired to the house, tired and happy.

Strange sounds, flicking light of fire-flies, the croaking of frogs and clicking of crickets, lulled me to sleep. Early in the morning, at about 6.30 am, with sun streaming through the fly-wired bedroom windows, there was a knock on the door and a tray was delivered and left on the tiled floor. It was an orange-yellow coloured drink with ice in it - a Djeruk Press. The Djeruk is a bit like a small orange but with green skin and makes a refreshing drink.

Breakfast started with a slice of papaya (or pawpaw), then cereal followed by toast. Bread needed to be held up towards the window and light to be scanned for weevils - little black bits in the bread which was baked from local flour. Flour was a favourite for weevils and they were like little black ants that had been baked into the bread. We had tea with breakfast and then a cigarette. Jackie smoked menthol cigarettes but the standard smoke was State Express 555 or Rothmans King Size which both Tom and I smoked. English and American cigarettes were luxuries in Indonesia at that time. Locally made cigarettes were incredibly cheap and clove cigarettes (kretak) were very popular with the Indonesians.

It had been arranged that I would stay at Tom and Jackie's house for about six to eight weeks before I would move to a house at 7 Djalan Taman Tjut Mutiah in the Tjikini area - about two miles or so away. The house was occupied by a member of staff called Weenas and he was moving to Holland after which I would take over.

Usen had the Bel Air waiting on the drive to take Tom and me down to the Kota (city) area of Djakarta where the office was, at 35 Kali Besar Barat, past the Glodok, Chinese district. The drive took just under an hour, depending on traffic conditions and I realised why a driver was essential. The journey was usually fairly slow and noisy, continuous honking from other cars, very hot and dusty, but colourful and very strange to me.

The dress code for the office was white shirt and tie, long white or grey drill trousers. Shirts could be either long or short-sleeved but a tie was mandatory.

The office was amazing - rather shabby, a single storey building like a small warehouse - open-plan except for Tom White's, the Manager's, office which was enclosed on its own. About 20 staff were employed, mainly Chinese but a few Javanese. The high windows were barred and several ceiling Kepases whirled and circulated the air. There was no glass in windows, just security bars, wooden storm shutters and fly-wire. Air-conditioning which was, of course, very unusual in Djakarta necessitated the glazing of windows.

The Chinese staff each had a glass of tea without milk on his or her desk with a lid on the top to keep out flies.

Morning wash - Djakarta 1963

James Fellows, Francis Peek's Tea Manager, took me under his wing and would be with me in the office showing me the ropes for about six to eight weeks before he returned to London. We were in the office by around 8 am or a bit earlier and we left before 3 pm or even 2.30 pm by which time it was really hot and humid.

On the way into the office in the morning overnight cables from London needed to be collected from the central Post Office. Very often it was me who called in at the Post Office for the cables and mail. Tukan, who had been at the airport to meet me with Tom White, was the general 'facilitator' in the office. He had contacts with the police, passport office and knew all the bureaucratic procedures which were necessary to arrange for obtaining things like a driving licence and wireless permit. He took charge of one's passport and all the photos which Colin Hammond had sensibly suggested that I had printed, and set about getting all the official papers which I needed as an expatriate European working in Indonesia. I filled in application forms for membership of the Box Club and the Djakarta Golf Club.

My mother's parents had told me that when being stationed abroad, you should leave a visiting card at the Embassy. This I did but I think the custom was dying out. It enabled the Embassy to know who was in the country and to send invitations to Embassy functions. The British Ambassador in Djakarta was Sir Leslie Fry, whose son Courtney I knew well and with whom I had been in the same House at Rugby for five years, joining together on the same day back in 1953. Courtney, known as Corky, used to tell us that if he had a bad end of term report his father would give him the cane. David Grant, who had married Rowena, my landlady's daughter when I lived in London, was also an exact contemporary of mine and Courtney's at school, the three of us all having arrived in the same House, on the same day.

My job as under-manager of the Tea Department (in effect I would be manager after James Fellows departed) in the Djakarta Office of the AIP was responsibility for the export (or in some cases local sale) of all the tea produced by the AIP tea estates and to liaise with Colin Hammond at Francis Peek in London which firm acted as the AIP's agent. I would also taste all the 'chops' or parcels of tea produced and report back to the estate should there appear to be any obvious faults in the finished product - black tea. Each estate had its own factory.

The sales for export would be conducted by Colin Hammond in London and for example he might have agreed a sale of 60 chests of Kassomalang BOP (Broken Orange Pekoe) to Elink Schuurman in Holland at a price of 3/8d a pound for shipment to Rotterdam. All sales, except to Khoramshahr (Iran) which were FOB (free on board), were CIF (Cost, Insurance, Freight).

A coded cable would then be sent from Colin Hammond as follows: 'May we sell Chop 192, 60 Kassomalang BOP at 3/8d CIF Rotterdam'. Before anything else could be undertaken to export this parcel of tea, a visit to the Indonesian Tea Price Controller had to be undertaken. His name was Mr Wasito and his agreement or rejection of the suggested price at which the tea could be sold was of paramount importance to the entire operation. I was in weekly contact with Mr Wasito. He would look at the leaf of the small sample which I would show to him and he would either say "Yes, OK" or "No, we require more - try 2d more".

West Java hills at Company weekend bungalow

A coded cable would then be despatched to London saying 'Regret unable for Chop 192 - we require 3/10d'. A cable would come back, either agreeing the price or making a counter offer of 3/9d. There would be another trip to see Mr Wasito. He would again say "yes" or "no" and only on his final agreement could the process to export the tea begin. Tom and I were invited to Mr Wasito's young daughter's birthday party on one occasion which was a very interesting afternoon. We took an appropriate present with us - a doll, if I remember correctly.

The procedure as regards the necessary calculations, bank documents, customs forms, letters of credit, booking space for the chests to be shipped on a particular vessel calling at the right port of destination, and all the other matters which have to be completed before a single chest leaves the quay (in slings to be lowered through the hatches of the selected ship by winch and derrick or crane) cannot be described adequately here, except to say that exporting through Tandjong Priok, the port of Djakarta for produce such as tea and rubber was sometimes not straightforward.

Banana Palms near weekend bungalow

One or two unexpected hazards and incidents which occurred during this process I may return to later on.

I was happily living with Tom and Jackie who kindly housed, fed and watered me and also introduced me to many of their friends in the expatriate community in Djakarta. Mimo Achesi, an Italian friend, would greet Jackie, bow, kiss her hand and say "Jacqueline - that is a beautiful name". Their garden at the Borobudur house was very lovely with huge blooming hibiscus shrubs from whose nectar colourful butterflies of many different tropical varieties took their nourishment. Malachite green, kingfisher blue and all hues of red and orange, purple, yellow and black adorned the wings of those beautiful insects. A 'tukan kebon', gardener, looked after the garden and cut the grass with a hand-held knife like a panga and swung it about cutting the grass on his haunches whilst at the same time smoking a clove (kretak) cigarette. He wore a somewhat battered straw hat on his head to shade it from the relentless sun. Cutting grass by hand with crude tools was a hard task but the Javanese accepted their way of life and practically never complained about their lot.

Very often on returning to the house by about 3.30 pm, heat and tiredness would overcome me and I would flop down on my bed and sleep for an hour or two under the cooling kepas, clutching my 'Dutch wife' - bolster.

Drinks were usually served at around 6 pm but sometimes Tom and I would slip over to the Box for a cold glass or two of Bintang or Anchor beer (the local brew - produced at the former Heineken brewery when Indonesia was known as the Dutch East Indies) which was excellent. Sometimes a game of snooker ensued but woe betide us if we arrived after the appointed time for supper - Jackie did not tolerate lateness!

I was quite busy at the office trying to learn as much as I could from Jim Fellows before he handed over to me. I had a very efficient young secretary, Miss Kho Lian Hoa, Chinese, who lived at a Catholic girls' home where Tom's secretary Miss Tjoa also lived. Tom, Jim and I were the only European staff in the P & T Lands Djakarta office. Several other girls also worked in the office, including Miss Dhamayanti and Miss Kitty.

The Chinese population in Indonesia was in excess of 3 million out of a total population of about 120 million. Although there are around 7,000 tropical isles which comprise Indonesia, perhaps only 1,000 are inhabited and in the words of one writer they 'gird the equator like a string of emeralds'. The present population now, in 2010, is around 250 million. So between 1960 and 2010, a mere 50 years, the population of Indonesia has more than doubled. This increase, replicated world-wide is a sobering statistic. According to David Attenborough, the naturalist, the world's population has trebled since 1960. This surely is unsustainable. Can the world carry on like this? I doubt it, but surprisingly, little is ever heard about over-population. This may be the most serious of all the problems which face our small, vulnerable planet in the future.

We worked on Saturday mornings but usually finished by noon. At the back of the office was a room in which rice was kept in large secured bins. Rice was given to the staff as part of their wages and this was because the price of rice on the open market fluctuated quite widely and by giving the allocated quantity each week, say 10 kilos per staff member, the price on the open market became of no concern. It was the staple diet of Indonesia. Some staff were collected in the Company Land Rover to bring them to work because public transport was scarce and unreliable. Others came in by bicycle.

Sunday morning at the Box Club was a chance to meet lots of people. It was a time for socialising with other members, their wives and children, meeting and getting to know personnel from all sorts of British companies working in Djakarta as well as other nationalities. A small ensemble of musicians played in the saloon like a 'Palm Court' orchestra and familiar tunes were a soothing accompaniment to the general chatter. It was a chance to catch up with events that might have happened in Djakarta during the week and at this time, 1961, events in Indonesia, unknown to most people in Europe, except of course the Dutch, were simmering. Holland was refusing to hand over Dutch New Guinea (Irian Barat) to Indonesia, much to the fury of President Sukarno. When Independence for Indonesia from Holland (after three years' Japanese occupation in World War II) was declared in 1945, Dutch New Guinea was excluded and was still under colonial control by Holland.

The Indonesian economy was in a fearful mess, the Communists were agitating, encouraged by Peking, and the armed forces were increasingly noticeable, buzzing around in trucks with rifles on display. When a column of army trucks came along a road, it was imperative to give way to them and it was wise to pull over to the side of the road, reduce your speed to a crawl or stop and let them pass by. 'Don't mess with the military' might have been the motto.

Indonesian paratroopers were being dropped into Dutch New Guinea and the Navy had launched an attack by sea. Tension in Java, and particularly in Djakarta, heightened during this period as Indonesia tried to reclaim Dutch New Guinea (now called Irian Barat) from Holland.

So there was plenty to chat about on Sunday mornings at the Box Club before lunch. There had been a couple of assassination attempts on Sukarno's life at this time.

People's children rushed around letting off steam. Two young boys who were particularly busy but also could be quite annoying were the Phoebys' children. Mike Phoeby worked with Harrisons and Crosfield whose office was situated opposite our office on the far side of the Kali Besar Barat. Kali means canal, river or waterway. Anything but free-flowing, the Kali by our office was practically stagnant, the water black, and there were log jams of sticks, paper, all sorts of refuse, even dead dogs floating, full of gas, in the brown flotsam and filth. This was not a pretty sight and not a nice smell. One should remember that public conveniences in those days in the Far East didn't exist and so canals (Kalis) were used for washing clothes, cleaning oneself and as public lavatories. People who were washing stood up to their waists in the water and swished their hands about in front of them and to the sides, splashing the top of the water to swirl away the floating human excrement from their bodies.

Poverty is a word used by people and politicians in the West about which they know nothing. I write in Norwich in November 2009 and have just heard Gordon Brown, the Prime Minister, say in the House of Commons that his government has lifted a million children in the United Kingdom out of poverty during the past few years. It illustrates enormous ignorance and is insulting to people in many parts of our world today who still do not have sufficient food to eat and live lives that give true meaning to the word 'poverty'.

At lunchtime Tom and I would cross the bridge over the Kali which separated us from Harrisons and Crosfield's office where we often had a light lunch. Hugh Thwaites, Mike Athoe and Mike Phoeby (all of Harrisons) and Jeff Dobson were usually present. Len Parris and Dickie Paylor were the Directors at Harrisons. Midjan was the cook and I have to say that the food wasn't that good but he tried hard.

Hugh Thwaites, Harrisons' tea man in Djakarta, and Valerie, a secretary at the British Embassy, were married in 1961 by the Reverend Beverley Coleman in the Geredja Ingris (Anglican Church) in Djakarta. Hugh later came to work for Brooke Bond in 1968.

Tom often lunched at the Box Club with other senior company men working with Unilever, Dunlop, BAT, Shell, the Banks and other British companies. The Kota where we worked was quite a distance from central Djakarta and so you couldn't just pop out for some lunch. The Box did a particularly good curry with delicious tiny, fried, dried and salted fish, something like whitebait. Occasionally I accompanied Tom and sometimes it could be a club sandwich in a small courtyard of a Djakarta restaurant, such as Mario's. The club sandwich was huge and had several layers about 4 or 5 inches tall, one layer with a fried egg in it. It was a favourite of mine and was accompanied with a cold beer, condensation dripping down the outside of the glass onto the table. We occasionally had a Chinese meal in the Glodok, the Chinese quarter, which was adjacent to the Kota where our office was located.

Jim Fellows eventually left for London and Weenas for Holland and the time had arrived for me to move to the now vacant house in Djalan (Road) Taman Tjut Mutiah - Tjikini district. Tom and Jackie had been very kind to me in my first month in Java and I was sorry to leave their house.

Number 7 Tjut Mutiah was a fine old house built on two floors. There was an open car port type garage for two or three cars on the left of the gravel drive, servants' quarters and the kitchen area beyond that and three fully grown tall palms on the right forming the boundary to the neighbouring house, which was the Swedish Ambassador's residence, and palm trees at the front facing the road. To the rear of the house there was a tiled area the length of the house leading onto a small area of lawn, a banana palm and various shrubs. A frangipani tree with gorgeous white scented flowers with yellow centres grew at the edge of the lawn. In the joint of a branch which sprang from the trunk grew an orchid. Orchids flourish in the tropics and giving a bunch of orchids to mark some occasion was not extravagance - it was similar to giving a bunch of roses in England.

Downstairs there was an open sitting room, a bedroom facing the back lawn, a shower and mandi room and lavatory. Upstairs there were two bedrooms with 'en suite' showers and lavatories and each with a mandi. Another small anak's (child's) bedroom adjoined my own with an open gap at the top of the wall connecting the rooms to enable you to hear the child if it was crying. A mandi was a square porcelain tiled bath, each side about 3 feet wide and containing water to a depth of around 3 feet. The whole bathroom area, shower and mandi was white tiled. The mandi was filled by one tap almost to the top with cold water which was not, in fact, cold but tepid, as the temperature in Djakarta rarely fell below 85°F except in the early hours of the morning in the dark when it did fall a little.

My company house, 7 Djalan Taman Tjut Mutiah, Tjikini, Djakarta, 1962

Floating on the water surface of the mandi was a small aluminium bucket the size of a medium saucepan which had a handle, with a wooden grip, fixed to the rim. Grasping it as you would a kettle with your palm upright under the wooden grip, you would plunge the bucket into the water, pull it out full of water and then tip the contents over your head. It was a wonderful way of bathing and I preferred it to the shower. You would continue sloshing bucketfuls of water over yourself until you had had enough and felt cooler and cleaner. A lot of water was splashed around but being in the tiled area, the water found its way over the floor tiles to the exit drain.

On the floor of the lavatory were bottles filled with water. The Dutch cleaned themselves with water, not loo roll. Loo roll was a luxury and was scarce so thin pages of the overseas edition of the Daily Telegraph served a useful second purpose.

Occasionally, after playing hockey at the Box, which was a ten minute drive from my house, I was so hot and sweaty that I would actually clamber into the mandi bodily and with the water pouring over the sides onto the floor I would submerge myself like an elephant or hippopotamus

Usen, Asmar, Minah and the cook at the Pavilion, Djalan Borobudur, 1964

in the water-hole, with my backside and back sliding down one side and knees up, which would just allow me to submerge fully. Ah, what bliss! It was the quickest and finest way to cool off.

In the sitting room upstairs was an old sofa with an electric push button bell attached to one of the arms. This was linked to the servants' quarters and kitchen downstairs. When the bell rang either Amat or Asmar, my 'boy' servants (father and son), dressed smartly in white shirt, white trousers and black kopiah on the head (a white kopiah indicated that the wearer had made the pilgrimage to Mecca which all Muslims are encouraged to visit once in their lifetime) would appear from downstairs. I might request a cold beer.

Asmar would fetch one and then approach the sofa, small tray outstretched in front of him, bending low so that his head was below the level of mine. He would pass the glass with his right hand, clasping his right elbow with the left hand, keeping it out of the way as it was considered 'unclean'. He would then withdraw backwards still bending low. (The left hand was never used to proffer goods or services.)

I thought this strange and discussed it with Tom and Miss Kho in the office. Miss Kho explained that the Tjut Mutiah house had been a Dutch household and that was the tradition, a hangover from colonial days and was still practised in middle class and well-off Indonesian families who had servants themselves. Miss Kho came to the house after work to speak with the servants and advise them that it would no longer be necessary to bend low for the 'Tuan Mudah' - young boss (as they referred to me because of my age, as opposed to the 'Tuan Besar' - big boss). European ladies were addressed 'Nonya'.

Jackie ('Nonya') occasionally came to inspect the kitchen area to make sure it was being kept clean as I believe she thought that I didn't take enough interest in the housekeeping arrangements in this Company property. She was right and her visits, accompanied by Tom, kept the servants on their toes.

A shortage of glass bottles was widespread and beverages such as soda water, tonic water, Coca-Cola and beer were bottled, not sold in cans. It was necessary to have the empty bottles and crate in which they were packed before any shop would re-supply you. You therefore had to purchase empty bottles and the crate. Supplies of soda, tonic, coke and beer were very important to have and I had an account with Toko Sinkudus to deliver direct to the house, swapping the empty crated bottles for full ones.

By the front entrance to the driveway of the house stood a brazier-like iron garbage container which from time to time was set on fire to burn one's rubbish. Most houses had similar arrangements.

Tin cans were prized and taken from the brazier by vagrants to be hammered into drinking vessels. You often saw people drinking from these re-cycled cans at the sides of many Djakarta streets where itinerant stall-holders were selling all sorts of luminous-coloured soft drinks, pastries and bread. A haircut at the side of the road and many other services were obtainable. Ice carts drawn by thin horses delivered large rectangular slabs of ice to customers. The ice was covered by sack cloth and the ice 'bung' wielded a long-handled pick to slide the heavy blocks of ice for off-loading.

Bread was hawked house to house by a bung (fellow) with two baskets full of loaves balanced and hanging down from each end of a springy bamboo and his cry of "roti, roti" - bread, could be heard well before he appeared. This was reminiscent of the set of 18th century coloured prints called 'The Cries of London'.

On 14 March 1963 I awoke early in the morning as usual at my house. At breakfast I looked into the garden from the upstairs dining area and everything appeared grey instead of green. That's peculiar, I thought. On going downstairs and out onto the drive I saw that there was a thick greyish-white layer of dust over everything.

It transpired that the Gunung Agung volcano, the home of the gods of Bali, had erupted with a huge bang. The volcanic dust from the explosion had travelled about 600 miles from the East in Bali and descended over the island of Java. The Gunung Agung continued its eruption for more than a month. It was reported that in the region of 13,000 people had died as a result of the Gunung Agung eruption. I wrote telling my mother in England about the volcano but she said in her reply letter that it hadn't yet been mentioned in the 'Daily Telegraph' which she read. News was slow to filter from East to West.

Glodok - Chinese area, Djakarta

An excellent book entitled 'The Night of Purnama' (Purnama meaning 'the day of the full moon') by Anna Matthews, published by Jonathan Cape in 1965, gives a graphic account of the Bali tragedy. By her account, 2,000 people on Bali died. Her numbers are probably more accurate than the perhaps exaggerated numbers which were circulated. She was in Bali at the time of the eruption. Bali's two other active volcanoes are Batur and Baturiti.

The senior executive of the AIP was Dakin Meyer, an Australian accountant. He had been appointed in late 1961 by the London board of the company to succeed Richard (Dick) Shaw as Representative. Dakin Meyer quite frequently travelled from Subang, where our Head Office was situated some 70 miles south of Djakarta, to the Capital for meetings with other heads of companies or for Embassy talks and would stay overnight at the Tjut Mutiah house. Before I had left Tom and Jackie's house, Tom drove me over to Tjut Mutiah to be introduced to Dakin Meyer who was on one of his visits to Djakarta. It was a meeting of the most senior (Meyer) and the most junior (me). This was a perfect example of the Malay 'Tuan Besar' and 'Tuan Mudah'. I was 21, coming up 22. Tom entered the house, followed by me, and called out "Anyone there?"

The downstairs bedroom door opened and there stood, much to our astonishment, Dakin Meyer, the boss, naked except for a towel round his middle. He had been having an afternoon shower or mandi. The introductions were made, Dakin welcomed me to the Company and he asked Tom if he could spare me from the office for a few days to allow me to pay a first visit to Subang to meet the staff there in the Head Office and perhaps visit one or two of our tea estates. Tom agreed that I should go.

By this time I had acquired a company car and driver of my own. It was a Fiat 1100, a small grey car with a gearstick attached to the steering column, which was unfamiliar to me. I soon got the hang of it. The front seats were in bench form, not separated, and there was a rear bench seat. It was a fine car and I was happy with it. The Company provided me with a young driver named Dedeh, who was available to drive the car at any hour, evenings included. The reality was that Dedeh would drive me to the office in the morning, hang about there all day, drive me to the price controller, or Tandjong Priok if necessary and generally be available, then drive me back to Tjut Mutiah after leaving the office.

Normally he would go off duty after getting me back to my house, but he would be paid overtime for any out-of-hours driving. Most people drove themselves in the later part of the day after work and in the evenings.

The reason that the Company provided drivers was that in the event of an accident which resulted in anyone being killed by a car, the driver would be imprisoned, regardless of whose fault it might be. There were many hazards on Djakarta and Java roads, not least the erratic pedal-driven betjaks (similar to rickshaws) which were everywhere, lined up like taxi ranks awaiting fares outside almost all public buildings and thoroughfares. Rubber bands tied horizontally under the chassis made them hum and sing as they were pedalled along.

On the chosen morning for my visit to Subang, I set off in my Fiat on my own. Dedeh the driver was never keen on going away for more than a day trip as this meant staying a night or several nights in unaccustomed accommodation away from his family, which reluctance was quite understandable.

One of my house boys, Asmar, son of Amat, my senior 'boy', would start giggling nervously if I suggested he accompany me to our bungalow up in the hills for the weekend to cook and generally be useful, and his excuse for declining was that it was too cold up there. He would say "Tidak Tuan, dingin, dingin" - no, too cold. Tom and Jackie kindly used to invite me to accompany them when it was their turn to use the hill bungalow near the Puntjak Pass. We used to swim at a beautiful public pool at Tjibulan. Punctured tyres on the bad roads up to the hills were common and tyres would be left for repair on the way up and collected from the garage on the way down. You never travelled without at least one serviceable spare tyre. We were all experts at changing tyres at the side of the road and could do it very quickly. You always carried your inoculation certificate booklet with you when driving outside Djakarta. Roadblocks were set up before entering a district where smallpox or cholera had broken out and your certificate had to be in order before you were allowed to proceed.

The car journey took about two to three hours to Subang through the Java countryside then gently ascended to a higher level where the foothills of the volcanic panorama began. Rice paddy was all around with large-brimmed, rattan–rimmed and dried banana leaf hats bobbing up and down as their wearers, mainly women, bent double planting out or attending the rice. The paddy (sawah) is a colourful green tableau, broken up by areas of palms and waving fronds of all kinds of tropical plants.

On arrival at the beginning of the Lands, rubber plantations were the first sign that you were entering the Company Plantation area. There was an air and feeling of order as you progressed towards Subang. The rubber trees were uniformly planted and reminded me of areas of cultivated willows which you sometimes see in England, perhaps grown to be turned into cricket bats. The canopy above the seemingly unending rows of rubber trees closed like a roof and only dappled sunlight penetrated. Little cups gathered the latex which dripped, white as ivory, from the V-shaped cuts in the bark. Some cuts were diagonal and the latex slowly oozed downwards to be gathered in the cups, not porcelain, but made from tin or aluminium. A rubber plantation is a fine sight and here and there an isolated car and a person in khaki or white shorts and white shirt could be spotted amongst the trees.

The latex is transported to the rubber factory on the estate and

Tom and Jackie White at weekend bungalow in hills, 1962

coagulates in large zinc vats. It is reduced to long strips of crepe, called sheets, which are shaped and banged into large, slightly sticky, squares (some 2.5 to 3 feet wide). The large squares of bouncing rubber sheets are then sprinkled with chalk, covered by canvas and stencilled on the outside with all the relevant details and description. The smell in the factory is horrible - a unique smell which is difficult to identify.

Subang is a small town, kampong (village) on the outskirts and then tidy bungalows with neatly trimmed gardens. Dominating the scene is the Head Office, a large white building on two storeys, pillared walkways on both levels with an impressive central staircase. The office was built in 1939. I quote from 'The P & T Lands' by W H Daukes: 'This building is without doubt one of the finest office buildings in the East outside the large towns'.

I quote again from the same source: 'In 1930 the Pamanoekan and Tjiassemlanden was considered to be the foremost amongst plantation companies. One of the largest rubber producers in the world, scarcely a superior in tea production with considerable areas under kina, coffee, sisal and tapioca and with large exports of rice'.

The world depression of the early 1930s and then the outbreak of the 2nd World War culminating in the invasion of Java by Japanese forces on 28 February 1942, resulted in a very different situation between then in 1930 and 1961 when I arrived to work in Java. In 1942 Subang was occupied two days after the Japanese invasion of Java, as a prelude for attacking Bandung from the north and occupying the strategic airport of Kalidjati which was on the Lands.

To clear up what may seem to be confusing I should explain that although the Company in London was called the Anglo-Dutch Plantations of Java, it had been renamed Anglo-Indonesian Plantations, but the Company in Java is known as 'Pamanoekan and Tjiasem' Lands. Pamanoekan and Tjiasem were originally two separate areas of land which combined totalled half a million acres and came together into British hands when Shrapnell and Skelton were registered as the freehold owners in 1815. Thereafter the Lands became known as the 'P & T' Lands and I will refer to the Java property as it was in my time and had been for all those past years as 'P & T' Lands.

When the Lands were recovered from the Japanese after the war and Independence was declared by Sukarno, they were in a very poor condition and many, being completely overgrown, were irrecoverable. An interlude between the Japanese surrender and the eventual recovery of the country by British and Dutch forces had resulted in a period when armed gangs of Javanese rebels caused havoc on the plantations and some seventeen P & T tea and rubber factories were destroyed and many of the houses and offices burnt down. When, finally, company staff returned they found chaos and destruction. By 1951 the company was back on its feet.

It had been arranged that I would stay in Subang with Robbie Robson, the Tea Superintendent, his wife and young daughter aged about 8. His comfortable bungalow set in a beautiful garden was a good place to stay for my first visit to Subang. I spent time in the Head Office meeting the staff - British, Australian and Javanese.

Opposite the office was the Company's 9-hole golf course, set out amongst bougainvillea and trees which I couldn't name. The ninth hole ended in a par 3. The tee faced the Subang Club and the ball needed to be hit high over a stream below, forded by a wooden walkway, to land on an island of green directly in front of the Club house. Members would be seated with drinks in hand on the wall of the Club house terrace, to watch the efforts of the golfers to pitch their ball onto the green in front of them. Some succeeded but many including myself came to grief and went either into the stream directly or after rolling backwards from the sloping edge of the green, much to the glee of the spectators on the terrace. There was no margin for error playing the ninth, but it was hugely satisfying to land and stay on the green perhaps for one putt to make a two - 'birdie'. I never achieved it.

Snakes shimmering like reflecting glass were often seen on the Subang golf course slithering across the fairway and also at the Djakarta course. On one occasion at Subang my ball landed at the foot of a tree. As I approached, I disturbed a small emerald green snake only about a foot long, and it slid past my ball and behind the tree. Was it poisonous? I don't know. Refreshment barrows were in place at the tee after every four or five holes at the Djakarta course.

The Company in Subang had its own swimming pool approached down a rather slippery wooden stepped sloping path lined by a heavy bamboo glade on both sides and you emerged into an open sunlit area, beautifully kept with about 10 changing huts and surrounded by lawn. Few members of staff seemed to use it, so when I went to swim sometimes taking a butterfly net which I had made from netting sewn round a bamboo frame, I was nearly always on my own and had the pool to myself. I always released any butterflies which I netted.

The Company also had its own hospital in Subang, fully staffed and equipped and run by two doctors, one British and one Australian, as well as Shirley, a British nurse. Before the war the Company ran three hospitals, distributed in different regions of the Lands. One was on Soekaboemi Estate.

The Club was the social centre of Subang and provided a well-stocked bar and two full-size snooker tables in a fine snooker room. Staff tended to congregate at the Club in the evenings and if I remember correctly there was a dining room area which served dinners on special occasions. The Queen's Birthday was a formal dinner event in Subang - black tie.

Company swimming pool, Subang

JJ catching butterflies, Subang, 1962

Black tie occasions in Java were actually black trousers, white dress shirt, black tie and white tuxedo but usually the tuxedo was allowed to be shed later on as it was really too warm to wear it throughout the whole evening, particularly if dancing was in progress.

On arrival at the Head Office early one morning Dakin Meyer asked me if I would like to accompany him together with the senior accountant David Atwell, to visit Tjukul Tea Estate. Information had come through to Subang that Tjukul had been attacked the previous day by Darul Islam terrorists and the factory shot up. Darul Islam was a faction of extremist Islamists, outlawed by the Government, who lived around the Bandung, West Java foothills and presumably had attacked Tjukul seeking food or money.

We visited the estate that morning which was very instructive for me and met the manager, Mr Mintodihartjo, who greeted us with tea and biscuits. There was a little damage, some bullet holes, but nothing that would interfere with production. After the visit we drove through the estate back to Bandung for lunch. It was an impressive sight to look across Tjukul - tea as far as the eye could see, a flat billiard table-like plateau of tea, all bushes interlinked about 4 feet high, interspersed with Kina trees which produced Cinchona bark (kina) and eventually the valuable powder quinine.

Lunch was at Dakin Meyer's favourite Chinese restaurant in Bandung - Queen's. We had Bintang or Anchor beer and on the table was a small saucer of little green things that looked like miniature cucumbers about three quarters of an inch long. Dakin Meyer pointed at the saucer and said to me "Try one of those - just put it in your mouth and chew". I did as he suggested and to my horror my mouth felt as if I had licked the red hot lava smouldering in a volcanic crater and I hastily grabbed for my glass of beer, tears beginning to well up in my eyes - watering from the sudden shock of chewing a green chilli. Dakin and David Atwell loved it - a green chilli for a green new boy! That was the introduction to my first Chinese meal. I have been very careful with green chillis ever since. The meal was lovely. Shark's fin soup was my favourite dish which often started proceedings. It had a pinky-orange colour.

My house in Djakarta was used by other staff members from Subang, either those who had business there or for those going on leave or arriving to take up a new position in the Company. The ground floor was for their accommodation. Normally it was a single male member of staff who visited whose wife remained behind in Subang, but very occasionally children arrived and they used the anak's (child's) upstairs bedroom, with mum and dad in the upstairs guestroom.

The electricity generating supply for Djakarta was insufficient to power the City at all times and there were regular power cuts. That meant no kepas, and in a fly-wired room very little air circulated. It was uncomfortably hot even with just a sheet over one's body. I had a 'Dutch wife' (bolster) in the bed and wore only a sarong. The 'Dutch wife' lay down the length of your body to the knees and you hooked one leg over it, thus helping circulate air between the legs. Sometimes in the night during a power cut I would get up, throw on a shirt and shorts and take my Fiat out onto the road and go for a drive with all the windows down. This was a good way to cool off.

I would be informed by Tom in the office that he had received notification that a Mr A N Other would be arriving on a certain day for one night and would require supper. That was fine and I would ask 'Cockie' my female cook to provide supper for two. She would come and see me at breakfast and I would supply her with enough money to purchase fish, meat or whatever for supper that evening. I was paid an agreed fixed sum by the Company for each meal supplied to a guest at the house. Breakfast was straightforward - fruit juice, papaya, cereal, bread/toast (minus or plus weevils), tea or coffee.

My lift van crate had arrived at Tanjong Priok and was eventually delivered to 7 Tjut Mutiah. It was good to have some of my home possessions again and I settled into the routine of P & T office life and the round of social activities after work.

One morning I looked down into the garden from my breakfast room upstairs and saw Minah, my wash-girl (babu), pick off a small twig from the frangipani tree, wait a short while and then carefully rub it onto the gums in her mouth. This surprised me so I asked her later what she had been doing. She grinned pointing to her teeth and said "Sakit gigi, Tuan" which meant toothache. It appeared that the whitish liquid from the frangipani acted as an analgesic. Dentists in Europe might be interested in that local pain reliever.

Golf was a popular recreation and having become a member of Djakarta Golf Club I played with Tom White regularly. We were both average enough to make it enjoyable. Our golf bags were carried by boys from the local kampong and they waited eagerly in the car park to get one's clubs out of the boot. Tom used his 'Peter Thompson' clubs - mine were 'Peter Alliss' - probably both sets by Dunlop or Slazenger. There were many water hazards on the Djakarta course: large water-filled excavations. Should the ball land in the water, the caddy jumped or dived in to try to retrieve it from the bottom and if successful was paid extra. It was amazing how often the ball was found.

Hockey, cricket and football were played at the Box Club and the occasional big dance evening was held there. St Andrew's night was a big event as there were lots of Scottish employees of British companies, particularly the Banks - Chartered and Hong Kong & Shanghai. For St Andrew's night a piper was flown in from Singapore to play the bagpipes. Riki Layton, of HSBC, used to do his party piece by climbing over the roof of the Club - a rather perilous scramble which he achieved without any serious consequences such as a broken bone or worse.

Kali (canal) Besar Barat by the Djakarta office, 1962

I went to Scottish dancing classes at the Club for a while but realised that I wouldn't be much use at it so gave up. My father had worn the kilt as a child and I am half Scottish but it didn't help me a lot in my efforts to learn the steps. I think Jackie had encouraged me to attend.

A drink popular with some members was known as a Bokma chaser - a glass of beer followed by a measure of neat Bokma which was Dutch Geneva Gin bottled in cylindrical stone jars. It wasn't advisable to drink many of those. No money changed hands at the Club. Chits (or bills) were signed and the member was given a monthly account to settle.

There were plenty of parties to go to in the evenings. Tom White spent most, not all, of his evenings studying by correspondence course for his qualification as ACIS (Associate of the Chartered Institute of Secretaries). I accompanied his wife Jackie to many of the parties which Tom could not attend. Tom threw an excellent party when he gained his much deserved qualification in August 1963. Usually the same people would be at the parties but it didn't matter. We were all young and enjoyed the drinks, music and general good spirits and smoking (no drugs, as far as I was

A kampong (village), outskirts of Djakarta, 1963

aware) plus the fact that we were all a long way from home and in a country which was known as a 'hardship station'. A Djakarta posting was supposedly bottom of the list of choice for ordinary staff of the British Embassy apart from actual Diplomatic staff who must have found Djakarta a fascinating posting in view of political events emerging.

Tom and Jackie knew lots of Australians as Jackie had a job with the Australian Embassy. Amongst them were Paul and Truda Olsen, Jeff and Jackie Jurd, Barbara, Max Williams, David James and John Holmes, Australian Trade Commissioner and there were friends who ran the Qantas office and engineers who serviced the 'planes in transit at Kemajoran Airport. Other friends worked at the American Embassy, as well as Hillary Shakespeare and Rosemary Roberts from the British Embassy.

During my first few weeks with Tom and Jackie at their house they looked after a dog for a New Zealander called George. Before going into the office Tom and I would exercise this friendly dog by taking it for a walk round the grounds of the Box Club. I believe it was a Cairn terrier. When George returned, (he had a room in our office, rented to the New Zealand Insurance Company for whom he worked) he would sometimes drive me into the office when Tom had other visits to make before coming to the Kota. George, who was not young, had a good sense of humour and on our way to the office used to point at the soldiers sitting in two rows in their army trucks facing each other, rifles between their knees, and used to say to me "Watch out for the melons" referring to the green helmets the soldiers sported on their heads.

The military were treated with caution as shooting incidents were not unknown involving roadside transgressions.

The Tea Department continued in the accustomed way. Flies were a bit of a nuisance in the office and I had a fly swat on my desk with which I despatched the unwary fly who might try to land near my glass of thermos-cooled soft drink. Tom and Jackie had advised me to take a litre size thermos of iced squash to the office. I used to put ice cubes into the thermos after filling it. This worked for some time but eventually it exploded one day on the way to the office and I had to replace the thermos. The lesson is - don't put ice in thermos flasks. Water was not drinkable from any tap, and all water for drinking first had to be boiled and then put in the American size fridge. This applied also to cleaning one's teeth - use boiled water only. Djakarta-itis was something that everyone was afflicted with sooner or later. It was an attack of the 'runs' and it was necessary to stay close to the lavatory should you be unlucky enough to be afflicted. You had to stay at home for a day and not risk the journey to the office.

One morning, samples of recent production from Tjukul Estate were prepared for me to taste. I detected a slight taint of oil on the palate and nose. I reported it to Tom and sent a chit to the Tea Superintendent, Robbie Robson, in Subang explaining that oil taint of the tea was a serious problem and that the burners which fired the tea should be checked. They were kerosene fuelled and Robson was not at all pleased with my report and the indication came back to Tom that I was mistaken. Fresh samples were drawn and immediately forwarded for inspection in London. Colin Hammond arranged for independent tea brokers to evaluate the samples and the reports back from them confirmed what I had suspected. The outcome was that the firing process in the Tjukul Factory had to be thoroughly overhauled and tea production had to be temporarily curtailed whilst the work was carried out. The oily taint to Tjukul tea was overcome and full production resumed. Tom had supported my opinion and for that I was very grateful. My original suspicion that oil had contaminated some production of tea at the Tjukul Factory was vindicated.

For a while I had been noticing a funny, unusual and horrible smell in the vicinity of my tea area in the office. Misnaeni was the name of the opas (general factotum). He was very small (ketjil). He did errands and jobs such as bringing round cups of tea and taking export documents for checking and signature at the Banks, which were situated a few hundred yards further along our side of the Kali.

I asked Misnaeni to investigate the smell and he set about the task, searching high and low for the source, clutching a handkerchief in front of his nose. Nothing was found until the big drawers of the counter where we kept the tea samples were pulled out. Misnaeni jumped back from the opened drawer shouting "Waadhoo, Tuan - tikus mati" - "dead rat"!

This may sound surprising, but rats were a very serious problem in Indonesia. Not only did they damage rice production but they were scampering around unseen in all sorts of places. We had rats in the office rice store - large aluminium tin containers were used for protection and Lai Boon Fah (Chief Clerk of the Tea staff) set rat traps in the store. These were not small rats - they were large ones.

The rat which was the source of the awful smell in the office had been trapped and died over the back of the drawer when it had been pushed shut, and with his handkerchief tied over his mouth, and holding his nose with one hand, Misnaeni lifted the putrid corpse with a stick held in his other hand and ran the length of the office and out of the building presumably to dump the carcass in the Kali. The incident had caused much merriment in the office, with noses being held and staff running away from Misnaeni as he approached, passing their desks with the stinking object. The girls were not amused.

When driving at dusk between our weekend retreat bungalow in the Pengalengan hills and Djakarta or from Subang, rats abounded on the tarmac at each side of the road. Their red eyes reflected in the headlights as they left the road on approach of the car. We always believed that the

A kampong, West Java, 1962

warmth of the tarmac after dark attracted them as the grass area cooled. There was a small bounty paid for rats' tails by the Government. Large painted hoardings with 'Ganjang Tikus' on them abounded - 'down with rats'.

One of my tea staff had Fridays off as he did some military training with the Indonesian Navy.

It was necessary at the beginning of each year to ask each member of the staff to declare their religion because some people tried to take all religious holidays and Tom and I couldn't remember who professed which religion. There were many Muslim holidays as Indonesia is a predominantly (95%) Muslim country and there were also many different holidays for different religions, as well as Chinese New Year, usually observed in March.

When President Sukarno was to give an important speech, the SOBSI Union insisted that we provide a radio in the office so that the staff could listen to the speech. This could last for two hours or longer. He was a great orator. On one occasion he announced that "my people would rather eat stones than eat American rice". The Americans didn't mess around - they halted Rice Aid for Indonesia immediately until Sukarno thought better of his remarks.

Kampong near Saleh's tea godown

The newly built Hotel Indonesia in Merdeka Square was the only new hotel in Djakarta, built with Japanese money allocated as War Reparations to Indonesia. The Ramayana Bar was air-conditioned, dimly lit, decorated with Javanese kerises (knives with ornately carved wood handles) on the walls, but even here, a rat would scurry past under a table, brushing a foot as it passed by, probably attracted by crumbs of biscuit or nuts on the carpeting, and this was a brand new hotel. The new British Embassy (built 1962) in Djalan Imam Bondjol was directly opposite Hotel Indonesia, beyond the central fountain and statue, features of the Merdeka Square roundabout.

Until the Hotel Indonesia was built, the finest hotel in Djakarta had always been the Dutch 'Hotel Des Indes'. When the Dutch were all expelled in 1958, the Hotel was renamed the 'Duta Indonesia'. This meant that all the crockery and the insignia used on hotel utilities could be retained. The old crockery still in use had the original DI stamped on it - a reminder of colonial days. It remained a fine hotel but very different from the new Hotel Indonesia. The Duta had an open-air dance floor with live band.

The other popular open-air night-spot for dancing with a band was the 'Wisma Nusantara', an elegant Dutch building opposite the Presidential Palace, and the Patti Bersaudara (Patti sisters) were popular young singers with the band there. Mosquitoes were a nuisance and burning dung coils produced smoke which curled from underneath the tables. Ankles and wrists were mainly at risk. The other popular venue for an evening out and drinks in the open was the Yacht Club.

As I was leaving the house one evening Asmar said to me "Musang ada, Tuan" - there is a civet cat. He explained that the civet cat (Musang) was in the roof and had kittens. He asked me if I wanted a kitten and I thought it was a good idea.

On my return later that night, Asmar greeted me with a cardboard box in which he had put the civet kitten. I put in my hand to take it out and it promptly bit me - drawing a little blood. I told Asmar to return it to its mother and siblings. The civet cat is not a domestic cat and the kitten's reaction to me was quite understandable - it had very sharp teeth and a pointed nose.

Musang coffee (Kopi Luwak or Kape Musang) is a delicacy known to coffee connoisseurs, especially in Java. Coffee beans are fed to the Musang which pass through its system and eventually come out at the other end. The beans are then collected, roasted and ground. I believe the resultant coffee is extremely expensive and prized in the West but in Java it was not considered a luxury. I don't remember if I tried it or not.

In Bahasa Indonesia (the Indonesian language) the word for the civet is 'musang'. Musang is described as a small animal of Java allied to the civet. Luwak (or Luak) is a relative of the mongoose and is slightly larger than the average household cat. I believe that Musang and Luwak are possibly different names for the same Asian Palm Civet. Nevertheless, despite some confusion, Kope (coffee) Luwak and Kopi (or Kape) Musang are the world's rarest and most expensive coffee. They are just different names for the same inwardly digested production line of coffee produced by the civet cat! I wonder if it can be purchased in Fortnum's or Harrods? It struck me years later that I might have become a Musang coffee producer but it never occurred to me at the time!

Tom White's desk was in the enclosed Manager's Office, the remainder of the office being open-plan. A separate section of the office was let to the Maersk Shipping Line of Denmark. Ole Caroe and Per Transo were the staff there. Ole was a large jovial man who smoked a pipe. Per was younger. I well remember the November day in 1963 when Ole Caroe came over to Tom and me in the office and said that he had just heard that President Kennedy had been shot dead. We couldn't believe it and were stunned by this terrible news. Everyone remembers where they were on hearing of JFK's assassination on 22 November 1963. I was taking three weeks' leave in England the following day.

Tom liaised with Subang and the Representative on all matters regarding Tea, Rubber, transport difficulties and oversaw the general smooth-running of P & T operations.

Tea was packed and sealed in chests. The chests were assembled at the tea factories with plywood top, bottom and sides edged with metal and internally lined with silver foil - details were then stencilled on the outside plywood panels with descriptions of the tea, its weight and country of origin.

The chests were transported by lorry or railway wagons from Pegaden to holding godowns (warehouses) outside or inside the perimeter of Tandjong Priok port.

Tea is packed in Java with a moisture content of around 3%. Being in the tropics, even though the tea is in chests, it is imperative to export it by ship as soon as possible to prevent it picking up further moisture. Excess moisture can lead to mould and deterioration.

P & T transport department lorries were hampered by a shortage of lorry tyres and consequently large quantities of tea were transported to godowns by rail. Railway wagons were rather like old cattle trucks, made of planked wood on iron frames and curved corrugated-iron roofs. Congestion often meant that the wagons would remain in railway sidings for some days and sometimes longer outside the port perimeter. Their destination before the tea was shipped was the Customs godowns inside the secured area of the port.

Tom came over to my desk one morning and said he had had a call from Customs and would I go down to Tandjong Priok to see them. Priok is about six or more miles from our office and before entering the perimeter gate, a permit is required. Priok was guarded by the army and was a high security area. The permit office was outside the perimeter

Our tea godown/Saleh's, Djakarta, 1963

and I needed to explain the reason for the application - visit to Customs - before the permit was issued. Payment for the permit was required.

On arrival at Customs, I was informed that there were discrepancies in the weights of some tea chests. The export documents, signed by me and the bank, gave the weights of the tea when packed. Customs selectively weighed at random some chests and found them to be lighter than the weight shown on the documents. So there were what were known as 'shortages'. These shortages could sometimes occur on the sea voyage or on landing at the tea's ultimate destination and would be subject to insurance claims. But in this case the shortweight chests had been deliberately damaged. On inspecting the chests we discovered that tea was coming out through holes and sometimes from torn ply panels, but consistently it was the bottom panels that were leaking tea.

On further investigation we discovered that the damaged chests were coming from rail wagons in sidings outside the port perimeter. What had happened was this. Thieves had come to the railway sidings in the night armed with tools, drilled holes through the wooden planked floors of the wagons and continued drilling up through the bottom of the tea chests. The tea spilled out from the holes into sacks or containers and off the thieves went to sell the tea in the market place.

I discussed the matter with Tom who reported the situation to Subang and a decision was reached that P & T would rent a godown on the outskirts of Djakarta where our tea which could not go directly into Customs godowns could be safely stored. Tom arranged to rent Saleh's godown. Our tea would no longer lie around in unguarded railway wagons but would be transferred to Saleh's. There were steel railway wagons, but not enough to satisfy demand, which of course were safe to contain our tea chests. Thus was solved the main problem of our shortages.

Some shortages were just accidents. Due to shipping congestion at Priok we had arranged through Charles Graham of McLaine Watson who were the agents of the Blue Funnel line, to request one of their fleet ships to anchor off Tjirebon (about 120 miles east of Priok) and the P & T would have the tea taken out by lighter (barge) to berth alongside the vessel. With her own winches and derricks the vessel would hoist the rope-meshed slings containing the tea chests, up over the side, down the hatches and into the holds. This went well until one of the slings shifted and out of it toppled one tea chest, splashed into the water, floated on the surface of the Java Sea and was last seen heading north to Kalimantan (Borneo). I witnessed this event and was given lunch aboard with the ship's Master.

Charles Graham came to our office weekly to canvas for our cargo to be shipped on Blue Funnel Line. (The owners were Alfred Holt of Liverpool). In 1958 I had spent a month at the Aberdovey Outward Bound Sea School in Wales which Alfred Holt had helped found. Many of the lads who were with me there were from Liverpool and sponsored by Alfred Holt, to give them some sailing experience and discipline before they began their seafaring careers with the Blue Funnel Line.

Charles was always immaculately dressed and without fail wore shot-silk cream coloured shirts with long sleeves, half rolled up. He was a charming fellow and much liked.

Blue Funnel was the preferred line that we used because they scheduled their ships to all the destinations which we required including Adelaide, Australia. Charles would keep me closely advised of the expected date of arrival of a selected ship which was due to call into Tandjong Priok. Our documents had to show the name of the ship on which our tea was being exported. Should the ship be delayed and it was then necessary to change plans and go for another vessel, it meant that all the documents had to be returned to the office from the Customs to be altered to a named substitute vessel.

Export documents Forms 16 and 18 normally had an original and sixteen copies. The first four needed to be signed by me, the remaining copies 'chopped' with a rubber stamp with my signature carved or fashioned on the stamp. A lot of paperwork was involved in exporting produce from Java - hence the number of staff in the tea and rubber departments in our office. The delays to cargo ships coming to Tandjong Priok were often due to Russian ships carrying military equipment to be discharged and also visiting Russian war ships. They all took priority and Port security was stepped up.

I witnessed a rather telling incident at Tandjong Priok one day after getting a permit to enter the port area. Continuing along the road from the permit office were the rice godowns on the left hand side before the port entrance. The rice godowns held imported rice from countries which grew surpluses such as the USA. Java formerly exported rice but was now an importer and as lorries bumped through to the entrance of the rice godowns from the road, overloaded with sacks from ships discharging their cargoes, some small amounts of rice fell to the ground and were gleaned by people desperate for food.

The surrounding perimeter of the rice godowns consisted of high fencing topped with barbed wire. Soldiers were posted at the corners of the perimeter. A girl, or young woman, in rags, carrying her baby slung in her sarong across her chest, approached the gated entrance and bent down to scoop up or glean what rice she could from the ground. She got too close to the entrance gate, so a soldier raised his rifle and from a range of about 200 yards fired off a shot at this poor girl. Fortunately he missed and on hearing the report of the rifle and probably the whistling hum of the bullet, she retired hurriedly, scurrying across to the other side of the road, the baby hugged to her breast. It might have been a warning shot and maybe the soldier had no intention of hitting her but it was apparent to me that soldiers could behave irresponsibly and were probably not accountable for their actions.

Kali Besar Barat, Kota

There were many desperately poor people at that time - beggars, disfigured people and almost naked men and women clad only in a few holey and filthy rags. They were painful reminders that we in the West do not fully appreciate how lucky we are. These scenes were not just common in Indonesia but I suspect in most Asian and African countries.

The journalist who asked President Sukarno what he had given his country 'except poverty, disease and corruption' asked a legitimate question.

Charles Jackson, whom I mentioned earlier in London, Chairman of AIP, flew out in 1962 to visit the lands and property. He stayed with Tom and Jackie and I was invited over to the house and then to the Box Club for drinks. I stupidly drank and spoke rather more than I should have done in front of the Chairman and was given a deserved rollocking by Tom the next morning.

Mr Jackson moved on to Subang after a couple of days. He knew Java well having himself been Representative in Subang in 1942, when the Japanese invaded Java and imprisoned him until the end of the war in 1945. He was a wonderful man, a real gentleman and author of 'Java Nightmare'.

Tom played football for the Box Club and his speciality was the sliding tackle, which led to plenty of grazed legs for him on the hard pitch. I played hockey for the Club with fixtures against the Indian Hockey Club who were very skilful and the Indonesian Navy, also a good side. I played up front and on one occasion collided hard with an opposing back and was flattened without knowing a lot about it.

Some while later I had quite bad pains under my left armpit and when I bent down or whilst in bed, could hear and feel gurgling down my left side. Being driven by Dedeh to the office and being bounced around when hitting potholes was particularly painful for my chest.

After seeing Dr Furlong and experiencing no improvement for a couple of weeks, he sent me for an X-ray which showed a collapsed (or punctured) left lung. This accounted for the gurgling sounds and Dr Furlong described it as a spontaneous pneumothorax of the left lung. It may have been spontaneous (ie no reason) but on reflection it also could have been caused by the hockey collision.

JJ at the Subang Club after golf, 1963

Dr Furlong advised that the cure was complete rest to allow the collapsed lung to close up naturally and the trapped air to leave the pleural cavity. It meant a spell in Subang for about three weeks in bed at the hospital under the care of Drs Chiswell and Graham, the Company doctors. Further X-rays showed gradual recovery of the lung which pleased the doctors who had advised me that if it didn't heal naturally, a trip to Singapore would be necessary for an operation to close the puncture. I was well looked after for three weeks in the Company hospital at Subang. It had its own X-ray machine. Happily all went well, the lung healed and I resumed normal service down at Djakarta.

Tom had made arrangements to have a Telex machine installed in the office connecting us with the London office in Eastcheap - a magical new technology. It was at that time state-of-the-art and a huge step forward in communications.

Tom thought that it would be a good idea for us to improve our 'Bahasa Indonesia', the language used in Java. (Variations occurred in other regions as would be expected in such a geographically huge area of islands). We had lessons at Tom's house once a week in the afternoons, given to us by a private tutor. 'Bahasa Indonesia' is basically 'Malay'.

Meanwhile the Company had decided to let the ground floor area of the Tjut Mutiah house to Lloyds for accommodation of the Lloyds Surveyor (of ships), Charles Richie, a Scotsman. He was a bachelor probably in his early fifties, a pleasant enough man but with a fiery temperament which sometimes exploded with his driver or some other unfortunate person who had annoyed him. I got on quite well with Richie but he more or less kept himself to himself. I once witnessed from my upstairs window his rage when his driver drove out into the road with him as passenger, and on turning right, promptly drove into one of the concrete bollards with painted arrows on them showing the direction to take. Richie had many drivers - few survived more than a few weeks in his employ!

I also played cricket at the Box Club. One morning at the office I received a phone call asking me if I would like to play cricket and fly over to Palembang (in Sumatra) for the weekend. It would be arranged by Shell and Stanvac (Standard Vacuum), an American Oil interest. Tom agreed that I could go.

A Dakota DC3 was provided by Shell and we flew on Saturday morning to Palembang for the weekend. I stayed with an American family who were excellent hosts and I think they enjoyed having me as a guest. It was very generous hospitality. A cricket match in the afternoon and then an evening party had been arranged and we flew back in the Shell Dakota on Monday morning having had a memorable trip to Sumatra.

I think the staff of Shell and Stanvac in Palembang probably enjoyed our visit and it was a change for them to receive a plane load of Djakarta cricketers for the weekend.

A vivid recollection of that weekend was having evening drinks overlooking the Musi river with a magnificent sunset on the horizon over the far bank of that wide river. I thought I was indeed a very lucky young man to be sitting there experiencing such a beautiful moment. 'Carpe horam'.

JJ, South Java sea, 1963

CHAPTER 3

The Riots – 17 September 1963

One of the world events which occurred in 1962 whilst I was living in Java was the Cuban Missile crisis. It crossed my mind that if the Russian vessels carrying the missiles to Cuba did not turn around, as the ultimatum to Khruschev from President Kennedy required, the possibility of a nuclear war was menacingly waiting in the wings. If that had happened Europe would probably have been 'nuked' by Russia and I wouldn't be returning to England. It was with much relief that we heard that Khruschev gave the order for the ships to turn away from Cuba and thus a probable nuclear war was averted - a worrying time for everybody.

In 1963 things were hotting up politically. The Federation of Malaysia was formed. President Sukarno pronounced it 'neo-colonialism' and vowed to 'crush Malaysia'. He renamed the Indian Ocean the Indonesian Ocean and proclaimed that the Greenwich prime meridian would be transferred from Greenwich to Djakarta. Also he claimed that an Indonesian scientist had developed and built a nuclear bomb - a terrifying prospect had it been true but it was only another example of Sukarno's wishful thinking.

On Wednesday, 17 September 1963, later known as Ash Wednesday, I was returning from the office, driven by Dedeh and our route back to Tjikini was via Merdeka Square, where the British Embassy and Hotel Indonesia, both modern and newly built, were situated.

For some days there had been anti-British demonstrations, for Sukarno had decreed that Malaysia was a 'British puppet state'. Around the British Embassy a huge crowd had assembled and there were gangs of men and youths pulling down the railings of the perimeter. A car was on fire in the compound. It was the official car allocated for use by the present Ambassador, Andrew Gilchrist, who had replaced Sir Leslie Fry.

It was a black Austin Princess - now a flaming wreck.

I have to say that I was alarmed to see the goings on at the Embassy but reassured myself that I wasn't anything to do with the British government but merely a civilian doing a job in Indonesia. The anger of the people was directed against Britain by taking it out on the Embassy, or so I thought. I was getting rather nervous. Dedeh dropped me at the house and I spoke to Charles Richie and said I thought that things would be fine if we just kept a low profile.

The telephone rang and it was Tom White. I was going to have dinner that evening at the Borobudur house. Tom told me that he had just got home, and that when he passed Merdeka Square, the British Embassy was actually on fire. He instructed me to remain indoors at my house and not to attempt to come over to Borobudur for dinner and that he would keep in touch as things developed. He told me that the Box Club was being wrecked and was on fire and that the mob was now outside his house. Stones and missiles were being hurled at the house and Tom said he was crouching behind the large sofa in the sitting room armed with a golf club and wasn't intending to go down without a fight. Our

The mob close in on the British Embassy, Djakarta, 17 September 1963

'phone conversation ended with the intention of keeping each other advised a bit later on as the situation became clearer. The burning and ransacking of the Box Club was a sad end of a familiar friend that had hosted events and been the meeting place for sport and social relaxation for thousands of people and their families during the many years since its inception.

This was not good news. I had my floppy briefcase with me (which contained my passport) and had changed into shorts. Because there was so much going on, rather than take my usual late afternoon nap on my bed, I remained downstairs.

At around 5 pm there was shouting and noisy disturbance at the front of the house in the road. I peered through the spy hole of the front door to see men, youths and even children jump down and run from lorries in the road into my driveway. My Fiat was in the Subang Atelier (workshop) having some repairs done and I had been allocated a replacement - a Borgward Isabella, with white porcelain steering wheel - a fine car.

In no time at all, the Borgward was surrounded, pushed from side to side until it was tipped upside down on its roof, petrol cap opened and 'whoosh' a match ignited the fuel on the gravel and it was on fire.

I realised in a split second that this was actually and unbelievably happening in front of me and my instant reaction was to grab my briefcase, run from the front entrance out into the back garden, scale the wall on the right, jump into the Swedish Ambassador's back garden (there was nobody there as he was away on home leave) and get myself as far away from the house and mob as possible. I had slightly cut my knee jumping into some pile of brick rubble in the Ambassador's garden and blood trickled down my leg. I hadn't felt it.

I was very frightened and had completely forgotten about Richie who was in fact right behind me. Richie did not follow me but stayed in the Ambassador's garden. I got out of the garden to the rear and into a road well behind the house. My main thought was to put as much distance between me and the house as possible and I ran fast down the road and away. I recall thinking as I ran - 'I'm only 23 and too young to die'.

After a short distance, I passed some single storey bungalows and in the drive of one of them was a car. Not so many people had cars at that time and so I ran into the drive. The front door was open and from it stepped a youngish Javanese man of smart appearance. I turned round and pointed in the direction of my house at the column of smoke rising some few hundred yards away. "Rumah saya, Rumah saya" - "my house, my house", I explained.

In well-spoken English my newly met acquaintance said "I am an Indonesian Air Force Officer. You are quite safe with me - would you come into the house please. Would you like something to eat or drink?" I declined with thanks. I explained that I would like to get away from the vicinity immediately as I thought that the mob might be searching for me and maybe kill me.

The unknown was the alarming thing. I didn't know what was happening in Djakarta apart from the fact that the British Embassy was on fire. Tom's house was being attacked, the Box Club was on fire, my house was also being targeted, my car was on fire and I was on my own wondering what on earth to do next.

My new acquaintance, the Air Force officer, told me that he would get his driver to transport me to a police station where he knew the chief officer and that I would be safe there. So thanking him, I got into the back seat of his car while he gave the driver some instructions and off we set. I decided to lie below the back seat in the well of the car as I thought that if I was seen I might be dragged out. What I didn't know at this time was that the riots against the British were directed against property and not the person.

I was worried that the journey was taking a long time and I hadn't poked my head above the car seat to see where we were heading. Eventually the driver came to our destination. A large sign outside indicated 'Seksi V - Polisi'. I didn't recognise the area and didn't know where Section V was in relation to the layout of Djakarta but it seemed to me to be on the outskirts somewhere.

I thanked the driver and tried to give him what rupiah notes I had with me in my soft briefcase - rupiah notes were often quite soiled and crumpled. He graciously declined my offer of money which surprised me. He said goodbye and off he drove. I was very grateful to him.

The chief police officer and his colleagues were friendly and smiling and offered me tea straight away and a chair to sit on. The time was about 6 pm and it was getting dark.

I think the policemen at Seksi V were quite pleased to have an Englishman on the run in their protective custody but I was very nervous that should a mob be in the vicinity who got to hear that an English person was in the police station, they could demand that I be handed over. These pessimistic thoughts were because I was on my own and uninformed of events which might be happening elsewhere. My imagination overtook me and I thought that I might be the only remaining English person in Java, everybody else having been evacuated to Singapore.

My hosts treated me kindly and then I thought it would be a good idea to make a telephone call. Who could I ring? I asked if I might use the telephone and a directory was provided. I would telephone the Kedutaan America (American Embassy) to tell them I was at Seksi V of the police somewhere in or around Djakarta.

I was asked whom I was going to telephone. I stupidly replied "Kudutaan America". The answer was 'no' and the telephone removed. This was rather disconcerting but the friendly atmosphere prevailed and I

British Embassy attacked, 17 September 1963

waited to see what would happen. I still had my watch on, it was dark and at around 8 or 9 pm, I don't recall the time exactly, there was some activity outside the police station and a police lorry pulled up. I was told to get into it, my hosts waved goodbye and off we set to I knew not where.

I sat next to the driver, with a guard with a rifle between his legs on my other side. I was driven into central Djakarta - all seemed quiet. The lorry drove into a military establishment. I believe it was the Headquarters of the Tjokroaminoto Regiment in Djakarta but I couldn't be sure. There were troops milling around - manned machine gun posts guarded the entrance. Inside I was greeted by someone with a clip-board. I gave my name and the name of my company, P & T Lands. I was asked where I lived and what had happened there. I didn't know the details except that my car was on fire and the mob were approaching the front door of my house when I fled. Several Americans seemed to be organising things.

The Americans were fantastic. Had I eaten, they asked? "Food and drink in there", they directed.

My clothes were in a bit of a state. I was dirty and sweaty. I was shown into various rooms where laid out on tables were clothes, underwear, shoes, food and drink. All this had been organised by the Americans within an hour or two of the beginning of the anti-British riots on that day, 'Ash Wednesday' as it was later known. The Americans had stepped in to help out because the British Embassy was gone, set on fire and wrecked. The only remaining undamaged part of the Embassy was the strongroom.

The Americans are the most generous people and on that day they demonstrated that they are our true allies and friends. They come to our aid when we are in trouble and vice versa.

It seems that all the British who had been chased from their houses including staff of the Embassy were brought to this one centre and then later on that night we were transported to the Hotel Indonesia where we were allocated rooms. I met up again with Charles Richie and many others whose houses had been wrecked, so we were all in the same boat, so to speak. We had a lot to talk about.

It was with huge relief and not a little excitement that I finally got to bed that night - glad to be safe and sound. It might have been a lot worse.

The Indonesian Army set up defensive positions outside the hotel and troops were stationed on each corridor in the Hotel - a show of force to demonstrate that the Government were protecting British citizens in Java.

It was certainly an outrage to tweak the lion's tail and there was consternation and anger in London that a British Embassy and 48 British houses in Djakarta could be ransacked in this manner.

Nevertheless nobody was killed - a few minor injuries, hurt pride and destruction of property was the price paid for upsetting Indonesia by the formation of the Federation of Malaysia. Most British wives and children were evacuated to Singapore. Dr Grace Thornton, the British Consul in Djakarta, won high praise for her untiring work in evacuating 166 women and children from the Shell Balikpapan Oilfield in East Borneo as well as organising the evacuation of Djakarta women and children to Singapore.

When the crowds had begun to form around the Embassy earlier that day, Major Roderick 'Rory' Walker, assistant military Attaché, asked permission from the Ambassador to play his bagpipes and proceeded to parade around the inside of the Embassy perimeter, bagpipes to the fore. This had apparently incensed the already volatile mob and later reports in newspapers made much of the bagpipe playing by Rory Walker.

In Geoffrey Moorhouse's book 'The Diplomats: The Foreign Office Today', published by Jonathan Cape Ltd in 1977, he describes on page 251 that Sir Andrew Gilchrist played his bagpipes outside the British Embassy before it was destroyed and burned on 17 September 1963.

I was certain that Moorhouse was not correct and that it was not Sir Andrew who had played the bagpipes but Rory Walker. Many years later I wrote to Sir Andrew at his home in Lanarkshire to establish the truth of the matter.

I quote from his reply to me in August 1990: 'I have never played the bagpipes in my life and have taken every opportunity to deny all bagpipe stories about myself. Rory Walker asked my permission to play the pipes and I gave him my full encouragement. When stones began to hit him I went out and pulled him into shelter. Provoked by this demonstration the Indonesians burned down the Embassy the next day. Rory (now married, 2 children) lives near Stirling and we see each other quite often'.

British Embassy on fire, Djakarta, 17 September 1963

This quote from Sir Andrew's own pen finally puts to bed any incorrect stories about who played the pipes outside the Embassy in Djakarta that day!

The Borobudur house had escaped the worst of the riots. When I had last spoken with Tom, his house was being attacked with stones but before any further damage could be done, an unknown person, but presumably someone with some authority, directed the rioters to cease attacking Tom's house and move off. The probable explanation for this, as Tom recently told me, was the fact that Jackie was employed at the Australian Embassy and an official Embassy car collected her from the house each morning.

The riots were aimed at the British, not Australians, and somebody in the area must have indicated to the riot leaders that they were attacking an 'Australian house' which would have led to serious consequences with the Australian Government.

Some eleven years later in 1974 Tom visited Java whilst on a business trip to the Far East and he returned to his house in Djalan Borobudur - it was occupied by the Governor of Djakarta, General Ali Sadikin!

The rioters moved away from the Borobudur house and Tom emerged unscathed from behind the sofa, golf club in hand. The servants, Tatang and Maan, persuaded him to leave the house for a safer area and took him past the pavilion (where I later lived), helping him over the wall and into the neighbouring kampong and then to the nearby Norwegian Ambassador's residence. The Ambassador was away on leave. Police at the residence then escorted Tom, golf club still in hand, along the road to the Qantas manager's house where other English refugees were gathered. Tom knew the Qantas manager and as it was Australian property it was regarded as a safe house for the night. The house next door, an English property, had been ransacked and burnt. The following day, 18 September 1963, the Police escorted Tom and the others who were in the Pegansaan district overnight to the Hotel Indonesia where I had already been taken the previous night.

The reason that Tom needed assistance from Tatang and Maan to negotiate the climb over the wall by the pavilion of his house to get to the kampong was that his right arm was in plaster. He had broken it a week or two earlier as the result of an accident at the party he had given at the house for about twenty people to celebrate his passing the ACIS professional qualification.

Some drink had spilled on the tiled floor of the sitting room and during an impromptu game of 'cushion football' Tom aimed a kick at the cushion being used as a football but unfortunately slipped on the wet tiles and went to the floor. Towards the end of the party he decided to retire to bed early, being in some pain, and as he mounted the first steps of the staircase he turned to me and said "Jon, I think I've damaged my arm."

He didn't appear in the office next morning and on my way home to Tjut Mutiah, passing Dr Furlong's Surgery, I spied the Bel Air, Usen vigorously polishing the chrome as usual. I asked Dedeh to turn back and drive up to the Surgery, from where Tom finally emerged with his right arm in plaster. Jackie wasn't in Djakarta at the time as she had flown back to England in June to be with her father who had suffered a stroke.

My car having been burned out, Tom drove me, after we had stayed for over a week at the Hotel Indonesia, to my house at Tjut Mutiah. The structure of the house remained but the internal fixtures, fittings and contents were smashed and everything moveable had been thrown down

Indonesian soldier during riots, 17 September 1963

from the windows onto the gravel drive where they were consumed in a large fire. Every light fitting, light switches, basins, showers, stair bannisters, kepases, and lavatory bowls were destroyed. Dozens of soldiers were being billeted in the wrecked building and many were asleep on the floor of my bedroom amongst the rubble.

On my bedroom wall was inscribed 'Usir babi Ingris' - 'Get out, English pig'. Storm shutters were pulled off their hinges - everything was gone or smashed to pieces. All my personal possessions, clothes, the lot - all gone. What a terrible waste in a country where the average person had very little. I could understand theft but this was wanton destruction. Sadly my cat, Spider, had vanished and I never saw her again.

Tom told me to send a telegram to my mother to say that I was OK and in good health as she would be worried sick as reports of the rioting and burning of the British Embassy were broadcast back in England.

The Communist Union SOBSI was trying to take control of the Djakarta Office and Tom and I went back to work there after a few days. The staff were shocked by events and individually they all came to my desk to say how sorry they were that this had happened.

There were examples of bravery on that day. The Reverend Beverley Coleman, who was the vicar of the Geredja Ingris (Anglican Church), neighbouring Dr Furlong's surgery, approached the mob who were closing in towards the Church and said "You can do what you wish to me, but do not touch the House of God". A rioter raised his fist to strike Reverend Coleman but others set upon the former, felling him to the ground and the leaders ordered the mob away from the Church. It appeared that the riots had been well organised by the PKI and lorries were used to help the rioters move from area to area. Forty-eight houses were targeted as well as the British Embassy and British Council Offices. Riots and damage to British property also occurred in other parts of Indonesia.

Bill Anderson, the P & T Rubber Superintendent, was stopped at a roadblock near Subang whilst driving his new company Chevrolet 'Impala'. He was told that as he was English, his car was to be confiscated. His indignant reply was "How dare you insult me. I'm not English - I'm Scottish". He was allowed to proceed on his way in the car unmolested!

Most British companies were taken under Government control and it would take a number of years for Indonesia to become respected again and take her place as a responsible country on the world stage.

During our unexpected stay as guests of the Indonesian government in the Hotel Indonesia, my room and Tom's were on one of the upper floors overlooking Merdeka Square and the shell of the British Embassy. There was an attempt by Indonesia to break into the Embassy strongroom which caused considerable concern. Those people like myself and Tom whose rooms overlooked the Embassy were asked by British Embassy officials to take turns during the night to watch events taking place in the Embassy grounds and the shell of the building. The strongroom had not been breached. As civilians we had no idea what information might be stored there but it was obvious that it would be a major diplomatic incident if the strongroom was entered.

Howard P Jones, the American Ambassador, was making firm representations with Sukarno that efforts should cease to breach the strongroom. Andrew Gilchrist, the British Ambassador, later received a knighthood for his conduct during the riots and his tireless efforts to

My house, 7 Taman Tjut Mutiah after the riots

prevent the Embassy strongroom being breached. Both Andrew Gilchrist and Howard Jones spent a considerable period of time physically preventing the Indonesians from entering the strongroom.

The shift watchers, including myself, Tom and other volunteers, were issued with night vision binoculars. Each shift lasted a couple of hours through the hours of darkness before being relieved by another watcher. A British Embassy staff member was stationed next to the strongroom and with a torch he would signal at regular intervals to the watchers in the Hotel Indonesia to indicate that all was well. Our job was to monitor those torch signals which were flashed at pre-determined timed intervals.

I remember viewing shadowy figures moving in the Embassy grounds and there was certainly tension in the air. It was rather exciting to be doing 'Spooks' work to help 'guard' the British Embassy strongroom and the night watch continued for a week.

After about ten days living in the hotel, it was arranged that I would move into the 'pavilion' of Tom's house, a small, neat bungalow in the grounds of the Borobudur house, occupied I think previously by George of New Zealand Insurance. He had returned to New Zealand and therefore the pavilion was vacant. It was re-fitted with new furniture and for me it was ideal. It had an excellent mandi and even a small bar.

The adjoining servants' quarters were occupied by the two 'boys' Amat and Asmar, Minah the wash babu and Cockie, the cook, all of whom had been with me at the now wrecked Tjut Mutiah house.

In the office one Saturday morning Per Transo of the Maersk Line asked me if I would like to accompany him by small launch (owned by Maersk) to the 1,000 islands a few miles out to sea off Priok. They were coral islands with white sandy beaches, palm trees and sparklingly translucent water. Amongst the coral reef were enormous giant clams, some as long as 5 feet, and in the shallows colourful fish and other exotic shells abounded. Per had obtained some Danish lager from one of his visiting cargo ships and we returned to Priok where we were approached by a monkey (monjat) seller. He had three young Rhesus (blue tummied) monkeys which he popped onto the table at which we were sitting. I said that I would buy the one with the longest tail and so 'Bimbo' came home with me to the Borobudur pavilion where she lived in a frangipani tree with an old wooden whisky box for shelter. She had a little leather collar round her hips and a long thin length of lightweight chain attached to enable her to climb down onto the pathway outside the pavilion door.

She was a delightful companion and would accompany me to a small pond in the garden between the Borobudur house and pavilion. While I sat in the pond with the water up to my waist, only about a foot deep, Bimbo surprised me by jumping onto my knees which were above the water and then climbing down into the water and proceeding to swim both on the surface and underwater with her eyes wide open. She was a champion swimmer. Until that moment I had no idea that monkeys could swim and this became a favourite occupation for Bimbo.

I found her a suitable new home when I had to leave Java. I considered bringing her back to England but I was advised that she probably wouldn't survive six months' quarantine as monkeys are very sociable and need company. Monkeys are known to be carriers of rabies. Doug Chiswell, one of the P & T doctors in Subang, told me that if you were bitten and the monkey died within a week, then you needed to come and see him quickly, but if the monkey lived, there was no problem. Bimbo never bit anyone. She was a delight.

As all my possessions had been destroyed at the Tjut Mutiah house, I was asked by the Company to try to replace as much as I could in Djakarta and pay in rupiahs.

I had provided lists of lost items for Insurance purposes to be sent to the Welfare Insurance Company in London, which was owned by Brooke Bond. On receipt of them Welfare cabled by return that I wasn't covered because losses due to 'riots' were excluded. I spoke to Dakin Meyer who contacted Brooke Bond and they instructed Welfare to cover the claim.

Many years later, items which I failed to list spring to mind, for example, I had a small Zeiss Ikonta camera which took black and white photos with a high quality lens. It is difficult to recall all your personal belongings when they suddenly have all gone. I was upset about losing all my personal possessions but I was thankful to be in one piece and I would be able to replace things gradually.

Uncertainty about the future plans for the P & T Lands continued for the next nine months.

My sister was getting married just before Christmas and I asked permission to take three weeks' leave in England if I funded my own return airfare. This was agreed and I flew back to England on 23 November 1963, the day following the assassination of President Kennedy. In my father's place I led my sister, Judith, up the aisle of All Souls, Langham Place in London on 14 December to marry John Musgrove, an ENT surgeon.

I left London on a cold mid-December morning in 1963 to return to Java and one of the Comet IV's refuelling stops was Teheran. As the plane landed I noticed piled up heaps of what I thought was salt at the side of the runway. The pilot announced that the ground temperature at Teheran was –4 C. I thought he was joking and I had not realised that Iran had snow and ice in winter. It was mighty cold as I walked to the terminal and transit lounge.

Back in Djakarta things were getting back to some semblance of normality and we continued to attend the office. Eventually momentous decisions for us were taken.

A supervisor from the Government was appointed to take control of the office and Tom and I were asked to reduce our appearances in the

*'Get out English Pig' - my bedroom wall,
Tjut Mutiah house*

Kota. Tom was in any case coming to the end of his contract and he flew out from Kemajoran Airport to return to London on 31 December 1963.

Those who, like myself, were still being paid but not going into the office regularly were told that on advice from the British Foreign Office we should not attempt to leave Indonesia as that would be considered as 'abandoning the property and estates' and therefore we should remain where we were until instructed by the Indonesian Government to leave. Government control of all British Companies finally occurred in February 1964.

Bob Milsted with his wife, Claire, came down from Subang to take Tom's place as Djakarta Office Manager. They took over residence in the Borobudur house and I remained in the 'pavilion'. Bob's responsibilities were shortlived at the office. Golf was played and parties still continued in the evenings.

In May, 1964 my work permit was cancelled and it was arranged that I should leave Java on 6 June. A firm friend, Alfred Elias, the planter from Subang would be leaving on the same day so we decided to begin our leave by making a holiday trip to Thailand, then Hong Kong and Japan.

In Thailand we were invited to the Royal Bangkok Sports Club by some Australian contacts and swam in the pool there. The chairs in the Club were covered in Thai silk - very smart and luxurious and I was doubtful about sitting on them and spoiling them with my sweating legs.

After staying a week in Bangkok at the Trocadero Hotel, we joined a BOAC jet to Hong Kong Kai Tak airport. By pure coincidence 'The Beatles' were on the aircraft from London taking up the whole of the first class compartment. The plane was greeted at Kai Tak airport building by hundreds of screaming fans. We were amazed and had never seen anything like it. We later saw them practising on a stage in the 'Firecracker Bar' at the Mandarin Hotel on the island.

We stayed at the August Moon Hotel, 25 Kimberley Road in Kowloon. Both in Bangkok and Hong Kong we knew various people who had formerly worked in Djakarta and been posted from there to Thailand and Hong Kong.

'Bimbo', my monkey, Djakarta, 1964

My first cousin once removed, Eric Udal, was the Legal Adviser of the Hong Kong and Shanghai Bank and he lived half way up the Peak. As I was returning from Japan to Hong Kong again I arranged to see Eric on my return visit ten days later.

Alfred's girlfriend at the time was a Japanese air hostess flying with Qantas. Her name was Fusako Ogawa and she was to meet us at Haneda Airport in Tokyo.

Alfred and I travelled on to Tokyo a week later and were met by Fusako at Haneda airport. We stayed in the Ginza Tokyu Hotel visiting the Presidential Palace grounds and then went by train to Fujiyama, staying in the Mount Fuji View Hotel. Fusako accompanied us on our visits in Japan which was a tremendous help to us because very few Japanese spoke any English then and Fusako acted as our interpreter.

We had had a wonderful and interesting time in Thailand, Hong Kong and Japan and it was soon time for Alfred to return to London which he did a few days after our return to Hong Kong.

On returning to Hong Kong, I spent some time with Eric Udal, made lots of trips on the Star Ferry back and forth between Kowloon and the Island and swam from the beach with Eric in Repulse Bay which I renamed 'Repulsive Bay' as it was very dirty with floating sewage.

I flew back to London from Hong Kong and began my four months' paid leave to which I was entitled. The directors of the AIP in London advised me that it was highly unlikely that the Lands would be recovered from the Indonesian Government and therefore they could not continue to employ me after my leave expired.

Mr T D Rutter, Deputy Chairman of Brooke Bond, when he wrote to me summarising the discussion we had had back in the middle of 1961 stated that 'should you no longer be able to work in Java, we will re-appoint you as an assistant in the Saleroom in London'. His letter to me started 'Dear Johnson' which was usual then in 1961.

So, at the end of my leave period of four months I made an appointment to see Jim Wernham and Cyril Dudley at the Saleroom in Cannon Street, London, in October 1964.

Jim Wernham's first words to me were "Where have you been?" I

A soldier guards my house, 7 Taman Tjut Mutiah, after the riots

explained that I'd been in Java with P & T Lands. Jim Wernham had also spent time there when he was a young tea man. "We'd forgotten all about you", he said. On producing my letter from Tommy Rutter, Jim Wernham said "Never seen one of these before" and showed it to Cyril Dudley.

Derek Wright was now in charge in the Saleroom together with Bob Hales and Peter Sawdy. They had all been in Ceylon together and were now back in London as Brooke Bond Directors on the main Board. Michael Gherken had also arrived back from Colombo. My letter was shown to Derek Wright who arranged a suitable day for me to return to the Saleroom.

I became assistant to the Indian Tea buyer, Tom Corley, with whom I got on well. Terry Porter was now Ceylon Tea Buyer and Michael Gherken did African buying. A lot of changes had occurred whilst I'd been away in Java. Jim Wernham, Cyril Dudley and Maurice Kember all retired shortly after I returned and Stanley Poulton sadly died. James Fellows was now at S S Smith, Brooke Bond's broker, together with Dick Bishop.

In my absence new trainee tea buyers had arrived - Nick Upton, Chris Andrews, Anthony Brown, Paul Champness and Steve Rudin. Tim Orgill who had been in the Saleroom in 1960/61, went to India but had to return in the autumn of 1963 due to illness. Whilst I was on leave I visited him in University College Hospital in London. On my return to Java I received a letter from his mother telling me that sadly he had died. He and I used to exchange letters between Calcutta and Djakarta and I was shocked to hear of his death in his early twenties. We had been very good friends.

I spent a day showing Clive Haines the procedures in the Saleroom and taking him to Plantation House to visit the Tea Auctions. Clive specialised in tea production and spent most of his career in various tea-growing countries advising Estate Managers.

I had a four month spell working in Nairobi to replace Derek Harvey while he was on home leave. John Webb, an old friend of mine, was in the coffee office and lent me his car whilst he went off on leave. Derek Watson and Barry Parton were the coffee men and Tony Moore was the tea man, under Derek Harvey.

I was lucky enough to see a lot of Kenya and also travelled to Tanganyika and Uganda, including Zanzibar. I spent Christmas 1965 and New Year 1966 in Fort Portal, Uganda on Kiko Tea Estate with Alfred Elias (and his new wife Sue) who was now Manager of Kiko, part of Agricultural Enterprises Ltd, for whom he now worked after our time in Java with P & T Lands. We spent Christmas Day in the Queen Elizabeth Game Park and had our packed lunch sitting on the Equator line, marked in white across the dusty red murram road.

Some years later Alfred, or Mark as his wife Sue preferred to call him, disappeared one day travelling on the road between Kigali in Rwanda and Kampala in Uganda. I was reading the Daily Telegraph one morning in 1977 on the train to work in London and noticed a small paragraph which said that a British Citizen, Mark Elias, was reported to be held in Makindye Jail in Kampala. President Idi Amin was now in charge in Uganda and I was very alarmed as Amin was an unpredictable despot and Makindye Jail had an appalling reputation for brutality.

I rang Michael McNair-Wilson, a friend who was an MP, to see if anything could be done to help Alfred. Micky asked me over for lunch at the House of Commons. I had known Micky McNair-Wilson when we had been part of a skiing party in Saalbach, Austria. We were friends and occasionally went to the Casanova Club in Grosvenor Square to play roulette. The 'Casanova' was owned by Pauline Wallace, sister of

British Embassy on fire, Djakarta, 17 September 1963

Christmas Wallace who had been in tea in India. Her greyhound, 'Johnny', used to lie stretched out on the plush sofas in the casino - he had won the Greyhound Derby and therefore had special privileges in the Club.

Micky made enquiries and was informed by the Foreign Office that sadly Alfred (Mark) was in fact dead, killed by Amin's soldiers and his body was never found. Some very bad things happened during Amin's time in charge in Uganda. He should have been brought to the International Court in The Hague, Rotterdam to answer for his crimes but when he was ousted from Uganda, he retired in luxury in Saudi Arabia. A disgrace. I remain angry about it to this day.

When he was on leave, Alfred used to come and stay with us at our cottage at Malting Green, Layer de la Haye, near Colchester and my wife, Glennis (née Barlow) also knew him well. Before he joined P & T Lands in Java where I first met him, he was with the Tea Research Institute in Ceylon. His death in Uganda was truly shocking and Glen and I lost a close friend. Glennis worked at Brooke Bond as secretary to the Finance Director, Laurence Green. We first met there in 1965 and were married in 1971. We have a daughter, Victoria, married to John D'Cunha, and two delightful young grandsons, Jacob and Joseph.

P & T Lands tea and rubber estates were no longer under British ownership and were now part of PPNB (Pusat Perkabunan Negara Baru), the large conglomerate of plantations managed by the Indonesian Government. I was never involved with the PPNB teas and was in Java solely to export tea grown by P & T Lands estates. The world was changing and I had had an amazing and exciting nine years working in the Tea Trade.

I had always been interested in paintings but knew nothing about the Fine Art business. I decided that the time had come to leave Brooke Bond and the Tea Trade and pursue my interest in paintings. I joined David Messum in his Gallery in Bury Street, St James's, then had many happy years specialising in marine paintings with Rodney Omell in Duke Street, St James's and finished working in the West End for a short period with Richard Green in Dover Street. Richard Green runs three West End galleries and is considered the foremost dealer in London. In one lifetime you can only scratch the surface of learning about paintings but it has given me an absorbing interest in an extensive field which unfolds in many varied directions. The media refer to 'experts' but I believe that you would have to live many lives in the art world to become anything other than a specialist. I was neither but spent most of my working life in two occupations which were both fulfilling and fascinating - the Tea Trade and the Fine Art Trade.

When I was working at Rodney Omell's marine paintings Gallery at 6 Duke Street, St James's in the late 1970s, Mr T D Rutter, now retired from the Brooke Bond Board of Directors, was a client. On his frequent visits to London from his home in Guernsey he used to enjoy popping into the Galleries in the West End to look at paintings. He got on well with Rodney. He was always most courteous and friendly and enjoyed 'Brooke Bond' chat with me.

On one such visit, he purchased a large, handsomely framed Victorian oil on canvas painting depicting a cliff top view of Castle Cornet in Guernsey with a large expanse of foaming sea below the Castle.

He said to Rodney, "Perhaps Jonathan could deliver it to my house in Guernsey". Rodney agreed and arranged for me to fly to Guernsey with the painting. TDR met me at Guernsey Airport then drove me to his house which was perched on a high point looking across the sea towards Castle Cornet, the very view which the painting depicted. TDR's wife was delighted with the painting. Their house was in a spectacular location.

British Embassy and burning Land Rover in compound

He kindly gave me a very good lunch at the Guernsey Yacht Club before delivering me back to the Airport. He told me that he loved going to London frequently during his retirement, especially to the West End, as he found life rather quiet in Guernsey.

After the confiscation of British companies and property in Indonesia in 1964 following the riots and Confrontation with Malaysia (British troops were involved in fighting with the Indonesian army in North Borneo), unrest in Java was still simmering and Sukarno was trying hard to keep the lid on things to prevent them boiling over.

The foregoing account of my life in Djakarta in the early 1960s, as I remembered it, can be summed up as 'interesting days in turbulent times'.

I had already been required to leave Java in June 1964, having been resident in Djakarta since November 1961, and so the events which followed in September 1965 were not witnessed by me personally but are well documented. I have referred to Tarzie Vittachi's book 'The fall of Sukarno' published by Mayfair Books Limited in 1967 for many of the details in the following chapter about the attempted Communist Coup, for which I thank him. The events which I have described in the following chapter bring to a close those chaotic days of turmoil which led to the end of Sukarno's Presidency.

Mob advance on burning British Embassy

CHAPTER 4

The attempted Communist coup – 1965

The beginning of President Sukarno's eventual fall from power began on 30 September 1965. He had not been well for some time and was suffering from kidney stones. He discussed with Lieutenant-Colonel Untung, Commander of the Tchakrabirawa Regiment whose barracks were adjacent to the Presidential Palace, that he had heard rumours in the Army concerning the speculative future plans of the PKI (Indonesian Communist Party).

The PKI were nervous about the Army and were concerned that the Army might attempt to take power should Sukarno's health fail.

Dipa Nusantara Aidit (born 1920, executed 1965) was the leader of the PKI. He was useful to Sukarno who used Aidit to foment unrest against foreign interests. The PKI could organise marches and anti-western propaganda quite quickly and these street demonstrations were on the whole non-violent.

NASAKOM was Sukarno's acronym to describe his style of government – NAS for the National Party, A for Agama, the religious parties and KOM for the Communist Party.

Sukarno was no Communist but he cleverly balanced his government by including cabinet ministers from both left and right persuasions. Sukarno thought that he could control the PKI by including the party in his government. The PKI thought differently.

He talked of Oldefos (old established forces) and Nefos (new emerging forces) and these acronyms were soon graffitied into slogans which were daubed all over Djakarta walls in the early 1960s. Large painted billboards with 'Ganjang Oldefos', 'Hidup Nefos' abounded - 'Crush the old established forces', 'Long live the new emerging forces'.

In early 1963 rumours about Sukarno's poor health were circulating.

A team of Chinese doctors attended him and the state of his health was to be one of the hinges upon which political events would swing during that time.

The events on the evening of 30 September 1965 precipitated actions which were to have such enormous consequences for Indonesia and for Sukarno in particular and they were instrumental in his long Presidency finally coming to an end.

On that evening Sukarno was addressing a conference at the Djakarta Stadium. After about an hour into his speech (he was accustomed to speaking for several hours) he appeared to falter and he left the platform accompanied by his doctor, Dr Wu Chieh Ping.

Rumours began to spread that he was seriously ill and soon people thought that he was dying or was even dead. It wasn't true but this was to be the catalyst for the events which then took place. In fact, Sukarno returned to the platform after a short interval and continued his speech but it was by then too late to prevent the chain of events which swiftly followed and which led on to the consequential murderous horrors.

D N Aidit, the PKI leader, was at the Djakarta Stadium that evening. He slipped away unobstrusively from the stadium possibly to make contact with Untung and he was not seen again until arrested in Central Java in November. Lieutenant-Colonel Untung, CO of the Palace guard, Tchakrabirawa Regiment, stationed at his Headquarters close to Merdeka (Freedom) Palace which was Sukarno's Djakarta residence, on hearing the rumours circulating from the conference at the Stadium, probably passed on by Aidit, assumed wrongly that Sukarno was losing his grip on governing the country.

The pre-planned arrangements were set in motion by Untung and his first step was to take into custody the top strata of the Army high command and this entailed lifting eight senior Generals. Armed Tchakrabirawa soldiers clambered into lorries to pick up by force if necessary these eight Generals and convey them to Halim Air Force base, about 15 miles from Djakarta.

Those to be lifted were Lieutenant-General Achmad Yani, Major-General S Parman, Brigadier-General Pandjaitan, Major-General Suprapto, Major-General Harjono, Brigadier-General Sutojo, General

Abdul Haris Nasution and General Suharto.

The Communist Youth Front (Permuda) was selected to assist the platoons of Tchakrabirawa soldiers on this mission as they had been armed and trained for the 'Crush Malaysia' campaign.

Dr Subandrio, Sukarno's right hand man and Foreign Minister who had been Indonesia's Ambassador in London in the 1950s, advised the President that up to twenty million Indonesians had volunteered to 'Crush Malaysia'.

The Generals Nasution and Suharto were not picked up that night. This was a big mistake with enormous and significant consequences. Of the six Generals taken to Halim Air Base, two were already dead, one seriously wounded, and the three others probably still alive. Having been blinded, their eyes gouged out, they were then mutilated, their genitals cut off and stuffed into their mouths. They were finally knifed to death before their bodies were tipped into Crocodile well, a deep hole on the Halim base.

Porch to my company house after the riots, 7 Tjut Mutiah

A shocking revelation was the participation of women in the mutilation of the Generals. It is recorded that knives and razor blades were issued to women members of Gerwani that night at Halim. Gerwani was the women's branch of the PKI. Gerwani was another Sukarno acronym: GERkang (movement) and WANIta (women).

The Djakarta Daily Mail, a reliable daily newspaper, reported that a fifteen year old girl (wife of a PKI member) was present at Halim that night. She gave the newspaper a description of her actions which are too horrible to quote here. There is no doubt that many women were involved with the brutalities which were to have such dire consequences for members of the Communist Party in Indonesia over the next six months.

At General Nasution's house two of his armed guards were shot dead. Inside the house one of his aides, Lieutenant Tendean, bravely put on Nasution's military uniform jacket and gold-braided cap, and purporting to be Nasution was thrown into a lorry bound for Halim Air Base. The deception worked for a while but was uncovered before arrival at Halim and the brave Tendean was killed. The lorries turned round and headed back to Djakarta.

At the house in Djalan Tenku Umar, Mrs Nasution tried to persuade her husband to flee but he insisted on staying put, wanting to protect her and also his young daughter. She finally urged him to go and in scrambling over his garden wall and jumping into a neighbouring compound, he damaged a leg quite seriously.

The soldiers fired their way into the house and in the confusion Nasution's little five year old daughter was sadly struck by several bullets, probably mistakenly, for it was still dark and the soldiers assumed that Nasution was still in the house. Having searched the house and not found the General, the soldiers left.

Mrs Nasution managed to contact, presumably by telephone, the Army Headquarters, informing them that troops of the Tchakrabiwara had attacked the house. She then rushed into the road with her seriously injured daughter and was transported to the hospital where sadly her daughter died of her wounds.

General Nasution managed to reach Army Headquarters where he found General Suharto in command. Suharto knew that a coup d'état was in progress and that some senior Army Generals had been abducted and that the whereabouts of President Sukarno was unknown.

It was with tremendous relief that Suharto greeted Nasution's arrival at Army Headquarters.

Suharto's avoidance of capture that night, which would have been followed by a horrible death, was fortuitous. He had been out all evening only returning very late. On approaching his house he was alarmed to notice army jeeps and lorries in the street outside his house which was not usual, so he turned the car around and made straight for Army Headquarters. On his arrival he learned that a political upheaval was probably under way as a result of the sudden illness of the President at the Djakarta Stadium a few hours earlier.

Suharto tried to contact his fellow Generals but could get no replies. News began to filter through to him that General Yani had been shot and that several other Generals were missing.

Nasution and Suharto realised that a coup d'état was taking place and they set about taking counter-measures. The awful news of Abdul Haris Nasution's little daughter's death devastated him.

Militarily, both Generals realised that they must secure all main roads and vantage points around the capital. The radio station, Radio Djakarta, also had to be secured. During the night of 30 September, Radio Djakarta had been seized by Tchakrabirawa troops and armed youths of the Permuda Front (PKI Youth Movement) and they intended to broadcast a communiqué called '30 September Movement' over Radio Republic Indonesia. So, securing the radio station was of prime importance for Nasution and Suharto.

Had both Nasution and Suharto been eliminated with their six brother officers, it is likely that the PKI leader, D N Aidit, together with Colonel Untung would have taken power in Indonesia and then implemented the planned 'Indonesian Revolutionary Council'. They didn't and thus failed the pro-communist coup in 1965.

Almost immediately the Army's campaign, led by Nasution and Suharto, against the PKI (Communist Party in Indonesia), began and was popularly supported. This support grew rapidly when the full details and horror of the murders of the six Generals became known. The dreadful news of the death of his beloved young daughter made Nasution determined to pursue the Communists with ruthless vigour.

It has been estimated, some say under-estimated, that in excess of half a million Communists were killed in the aftermath of the failed coup. The Chinese, of whom there were around three million living in Indonesia, also suffered persecution. Even in Bali, known for its tranquillity and beauty, also in Makassar and Sumatra, the witch hunt against Communists was pursued. It has been estimated that fifty thousand people, including women and children, were slaughtered in Bali alone, and most Chinese completely eliminated.

This holocaust in Indonesia in the five months following the attempted but failed coup in September 1965 went almost unnoticed in the outside world, mainly because Indonesia at that time was very experienced in banning foreign correspondents and also because communications with the rest of the world were always very difficult in the early and mid 1960s.

More people died in Indonesia in the five months after the failed coup than had died during the American Civil War of 1861–1865. The number of American dead in the four years of that conflict was estimated to be around 600,000.

It is almost unbelievable that such violence and brutality could occur in a country like Indonesia, whose people are generally kind and happy.

C L Sulzberger of the New York Times summed it up perceptively: 'Indonesians are gentle and instinctively polite, but hidden behind their smiles is that strange Malay streak, that inner frenzied bloodlust which has given to other languages one of their few Malay words – amok'.

On 11 March 1966 General Suharto was finally given executive authority signed by President Sukarno to ban the Communist Party and also confirming the death sentence which had been previously passed on Colonel Untung. D N Aidit had been executed by an Army firing squad on 22 November 1965.

Sukarno was now President in name only and was ultimately succeeded by Suharto who became the next President of Indonesia. A very different situation might now prevail had the failed coup brought Untung and Aidit to power. The fate of a nation hangs on very thin threads.

A Prahu off Java